BAKER STUDIES IN BIBLICAL ARCHAEOLOGY

THE NAG HAMMADI
GNOSTIC TEXTS
AND THE BIBLE

BAKER STUDIES IN BIBLICAL ARCHAEOLOGY

THE NAG HAMMADI GNOSTIC TEXTS AND THE BIBLE

by

Andrew K. Helmbold

BAKER BOOK HOUSE
Grand Rapids, Michigan
1967

CONTENTS

I.	New Gnostic Texts	11
II.	The Hydra-headed Heresy	23
III.	The Jung Codex (Codex I)	32
IV.	The Gospel of Truth	38
V.	The Apocryphon of John	45
VI.	The Gospel of Thomas	55
VII.	The Gospel of Philip	64
VIII.	The Remainder of Codex II	72
IX.	Codex V	79
X.	Gnosticism and Biblical Studies	88
	Glossary	97
	Index of Subjects	100
	Index of Scripture Passages	105

ILLUSTRATIONS

Map of Ancient Egypt 10

Site of the Manuscript Discovery 12
Photo by Jean Doresse

Graeco-Roman Cemetery 13
Photo by James M. Robinson

A Sixth-Dynasty Tomb 13
Photo by James M. Robinson

Nag Hammadi Gnostic Codices 33
Photo by Jean Doresse

Jean Doresse and Toga Mina 36
Photo by Jean Doresse

A Page from the Gospel of Truth 39
Courtesy, Rascher & Cie, Verlag

Codex II, Half Opened 46
Courtesy, Deutsches Archaeologische Institut

Codex II, Reverse Side 47
Courtesy, Deutsches Archaeologische Institut

Editors at Work on the Gospel of Thomas 56
Courtesy, E. J. Brill and editors

The Gospel of Thomas and the Gospel of Philip 65
Photo by Jean Doresse

The Untitled Work of Codex II 74
Courtesy, Deutsches Archaeologische Institut

PREFACE

The second century A.D. has been a comparatively obscure period in church history. We do know that two important aspects of that century were the rise of Gnosticism as a threat to the orthodoxy of the church, and the resultant struggle which is portrayed by the apologists, beginning with Justin Martyr and Irenaeus. Now, through the discovery of the Nag Hammadi Gnostic texts, we know first hand what the Gnostics believed and why their beliefs were a danger to orthodox Christianity. A study of these texts leads one into many linguistic, historical, hermeneutical, and theological bypaths. In this volume an attempt is made to point up the basic ideas in the texts and then evaluate those ideas on the grounds of their value to Biblical and theological students today. No attempt has been made to be exhaustive, but rather to point out general directions.

Since seminary days, two decades ago, the author has been interested in Gnosticism. When the Nag Hammadi find became known in America, he immediately set to work on the Coptic texts. In his research he has benefited, directly or indirectly, from the labors of a host of scholars specializing in Gnosticism, Biblical interpretation, church history, the Coptic language and literature, etc. Some of his indebtedness can be seen in the footnotes and bibliographies, but these by no means exhaust the list of those whose work has contributed to the author's understanding of these texts.

The author has relied on his own translation of the Coptic texts of Codex II (except the *Gospel of Thomas*) and Codex V. Where translations were available, he has compared his own work with that of other scholars. He has worked from the standard translations of *Thomas* and the *Gospel of Truth*. Unfortunately, two texts — *De Resurrectione* and part of the untitled work of Codex II — were not accessible, so for them and for unpublished texts the author has been dependent upon the comments of others.

The bibliographies appended to each chapter are limited to titles in English, except where necessity ruled otherwise. These lists are not intended to be exhaustive, but suggestive. In dealing with individual texts, one should consult the general works cited at the end of the first three chapters since there is no repetition of titles. A careful study of the footnotes will give other leads for additional research sources.

Grateful acknowledgment must be made of the kindness of several individuals and firms: A. R. Mowbray & Co., London, gave permission to quote from *The Jung Codex,* page 29. E. J. Brill, Ltd., Leiden, provided the photo used on page 56 which originally appeared in *Brill's News,* 1960, and is used by courtesy of the authors whose names appear beneath the picture. Rascher Verlag, Zurich, kindly provided a number of plates from the text of *Evangelium Veritatis,* one of which is reproduced on page 39. M. Jean Doresse has kindly shared four photos, three of which were first published in his work *The Secret Books of the Egyptian Gnostics.* These pictures are reproduced on pages 12, 33, 36, and 65. James M. Robinson graciously provided two pictures of the site of the discovery, which are found on page 13. Martin Krause, Pahor Labib, and the Deutsches Archaeologische Institut provided three pictures which first appeared in *Die Drei Versionem . . . A. J.* and are reproduced on pages 46, 47, and 74. The map used in the frontispiece is reproduced, with variations, from a previous work in this monograph series — Dr. Charles F. Pfeiffer's *Tell el-Amarna and the Bible.*

The author would also acknowledge his gratitude to the libraries which have placed their facilities at his disposal, especially the libraries at Eastern Baptist Seminary, Philadelphia, and Union Theological Seminary, Richmond. He would also record his indebtedness to Dr. Pfeiffer for his encouragement and assistance, and to the staff of Baker Book House for careful supervision of technical details. Most of all, he would point out that the careful and critical reading of the manuscript by his wife Helen has contributed immeasurably to its clarity. Without her help and encouragement the book might have "died aborning."

With the hope that this work will serve as an introduction to the study of these ancient Gnostic manuscripts, and that, above all, it will lead the reader to an increased appreciation of the Scriptures and a deeper devotion to the faith therein revealed, the author sends forth this volume.

Andrew K. Helmbold

Frederick College
Portsmouth, Virginia

ABBREVIATIONS

A.J. or *Apoc. John: The Apocryphon of John*

B.A.: Biblical Archaeologist

B.E.T.S.: Bulletin of the Evangelical Theological Society

BG.: Codex Berolinensis 8502

B.J.R.L.: Bulletin of the John Rylands Library

CGP.I: Coptic Gnostic Papyri in the Coptic Museum at Old Cairo,
   Vol. I

E.V.: The Gospel of Truth (Evangelium Veritatis)

J.B.L.: Journal of Biblical Literature

J.E.H.: Journal of Ecclesiastical History

J.N.E.S.: Journal of Near Eastern Studies

J.T.S.: Journal of Theological Studies

N.T. Apoc.: New Testament Apocrypha, ed. Hennecke and Schneemelcher, Eng. tr. Robert McL. Wilson

S.J.Th.: Scottish Journal of Theology

TLZ: Theologische Literaturzeitung

V.C.: Vigilae Christianae

Z.K.G.: Zeitschrift fur Kirchengeschichte

Z.R.G.: Zeitschrift fur Religionsgeschichte

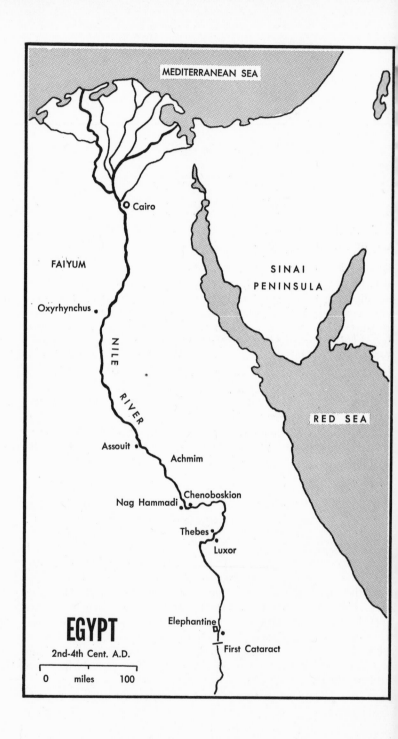

NEW GNOSTIC TEXTS

A. THE DISCOVERY AND ITS EXTENT

In 1945 some Egyptian peasants, digging in an old cave for bird manure to enrich their fields, made a discovery that has enriched the scholarly world and produced a harvest of knowledge concerning a movement that contended with Christianity for supremacy in the second-fourth centuries. In a large jar these peasants discovered thirteen codices (hand-written manuscripts in book form), which had evidently been collected by a group of Gnostics or someone interested in the movement. The story of the manuscripts from that day to this has been an interesting one involving intrigue, claims and counter-claims, war and strife. Now, nearly twenty years after the discovery was first made public, and after only a fraction of the texts have been translated and published, enough material is at hand to attempt a survey of what has been discovered and what the scholars have made of it.

The site of the discovery was the eastern face of the steep cliffs of Jebel et Tarif, not far from Shenesit, Chenoboskion, the site of St. Pachomius' famous monastery. Here, sixty miles downstream from Luxor, the Nile makes a great bend. On the western bank is the town of Nag'-Hammadi. Amid fields of sugar cane, the villages of Debba, Es-Sayyad and El Qasr occupy the river valley on the eastern bank. The limestone cliffs face the bend to the south, and turn northward to face the east. Here, near the village of Hamra-Doum, a cemetery had been located in the face of the limestone rock. The tombs highest up were of local rulers of the sixth dynasty (ca. 2300 B.C.), while those lower were from the Graeco-Roman period. In one of the cave-tombs the peasants found the large jar which, when broken, disgorged its library of Gnostic works.

As has happened before (cf. Tischendorf at Mount Sinai), the ignorance of the peasants resulted in tragedy, for they

Site of the Manuscript Discovery. The Nag Hammadi manuscripts were found at the base of Jebel et Tarif in a recess or carved-out tomb.

tore up, burned, or otherwise destroyed some pages of the codices, thinking they were of no value. What remained was sold for three Egyptian pounds (about one dollar). They were brought to Cairo and acquired by three purchasers. Sometime in 1946 one codex (Codex I), with some leaves missing, due, in all probability, to mishandling, was bought by a second-hand dealer, now deceased. A second codex (Codex IV) was bought for the Coptic Museum by its director, Toga Mina, who lamentably died before the Museum could acquire all the manuscripts. The whereabouts of the other eleven codices from 1946 to 1949 seems to be shrouded in obscurity. By 1949 a dealer succeeded in acquiring the eleven and had an expert appraisal made of them.[1] After protracted negotiations with this dealer, Mlle. Dattari, during which the Egyptian government forbade their exportation, the government seized the codices in 1952, paying the dealer the sum of fifty thousand Egyptian pounds.

---

[1]Jean Doresse, *Les livres sécrets des Gnostiques d'Égypte* (Paris, Libraire Plon, 1958), p. 139.

Graeco-Roman Cemetery at the Foot of Jebel et-Tarif. The site of the manuscript find is in the vicinity of the large broken stone visible in this picture.

A Sixth-Dynasty Tomb. One of a number of tombs located on the face of the cliff of Jebel et Tarif.

Thus twelve of the thirteen codices came into the possession o
the Coptic Museum at Cairo. The story of the other code
will be recounted in a subsequent chapter.[2]

Over-all, the codices are in an excellent state of preservation
Four of them are virtually intact, six are almost complete, tw
are very fragmentary, and the final one (the Jung Codex, No
I[3]) has considerable lacunae. Eleven of the thirteen still re
tained their original soft leather bindings that resemble moder
brief cases tied with leather thongs. Twelve of the codices var
14 to 15 centimeters (about 5½ to 6 inches) wide by 25 to 2
centimeters (about 9¾ to 11¼ inches) high. Codex II is the mos
beautiful and voluminous of the find, measuring 21 centimeter
(8¼ inches) by 27 centimeters (10½ inches). It contains 17
pages with a maximum of thirty-seven lines per page. The tota
find has about one thousand pages, of which nearly eight hun
dred are in good condition.

The codices were all written in Coptic script, albeit using
many Greek words.[4] The single-column pages of most codice
are covered with writing of regularity, clarity, and beauty. The
Jung Codex is the least outstanding in regard to handwriting
while Codex II is the best. Altogether, Dr. Puech describes the
find as the best in appearance of any Greek or Coptic papyr
thus far recovered.[5] Linguistically, ten of the codices have bee
classified as being written in the Sahidic dialect, two more in a
new or unknown dialect (probably Sahidic with influences from
Achmimic and Sub-Achmimic), while the Jung Codex is Sub-
Achmimic. This dialect belonged to middle Egypt, the area
about Assiout, north of Achmim, thus placing the writing of
this codex in the area where it was found. The other codices
therefore, were either written elsewhere or were written by
scribes who came to Chenoboskion from other sections of
Egypt. However, the linguistic evidence presented by the works

---

[2]Cf. *infra,* III, pp. 32, 33.

[3]Cf. *infra,* pg. 33.

[4]Coptic is the language of ancient Egypt written in Greek capital letters with
  the addition of six letters from the latest stage of Egyptian (Demotic) for
  sounds not in Greek. There are four principal dialects: Sahidic, Achmimic,
  Sub-Achmimic, and Bohairic. The latter continued in use down to modern
  times as the liturgical language of the Coptic Church. The language came
  into existence around 200 A.D. (some think as a means of translating the
  Bible into the vernacular), and held sway until displaced by Arabic in the
  period from A.D. 700 to 900. For a study of its importance to Biblical studies
  see Walter Till, "Coptic and Its Value," *B.J.R.L.,* XL (1957), pp. 228-258.

[5]Henri-Charles Puech, "The Jung Codex and other Gnostic Documents," *The
  Jung Codex,* trans. and ed. F. L. Cross, p. 17.

hus far published shows that there are Greek originals behind hem all, and possibly a Syriac or Aramaic original behind the Greek of one work, the *Gospel of Thomas.* This leads to the conclusion that the codices represent an attempt to make available to the common man of the fourth-fifth century A.D. in middle Egypt the original works of the Gnostic thinkers that were composed, in all probability, more than two hundred years earlier. Further consideration of the dates of original composition of the various works will be found in the chapters dealing with each of them.

Coming now to a catalog of the contents of the thirteen codices, we find confusion compounded. This is not because scholars are ignorant of what treatises were in them, but because at least four systems of numbering have appeared. Since three of these are being used extensively, they will be given below. However, it seems that the one used by the Coptic Museum should become standard.[6] The second system, by Jean Doresse,[7] and a third, by Dr. Henri-Charles Puech,[8] will be given in parentheses. Dr. Walter Till in his edition of Berlin Codex 8502[9] has used a fourth system in referring to variant texts of the *Apocryphon of John* in the Nag Hammadi codices. Further confusion arises because the Coptic Museum began the publication of photographic reproductions of the texts, calling the first volume *Coptic Gnostic Papyri in the Coptic Museum at Old Cairo, Vol. I,* although it contains 112 of the 175 pages of Codex II.

Before presenting the formal catalog of the codices and their contents, it should be pointed out that Doresse and Krause list forty-nine separate treatises, while Puech lists forty-eight. These fall into such categories as apocryphal and pseudepigraphical gospels, acts, and epistles (not identical with those previously known and commonly listed in these categories), apocryphons, apocalypses, doctrinal treatises, cosmogonies, Hermetic works, etc. All are more or less directly Gnostic.

---

[6]Martin Krause, "Der koptische Hanschriftenfund bei Nag Hammadi," *Mitteilungen des Deutschen Archäologischen Instituts Abteilung Kairo, Band* 18 (Wiesbaden: Harrassowitz, 1962).

[7]*Op. cit.,* pp. 165-167.

[8]"Les Nouxeaux Écrits Gnostiques découverts en Haute-Égypte," *Coptic Studies in Honor of Walter Ewing Crum,* ed. Michel Malinine (*Bulletin of the Byzantine Institute*) (Boston: 1950), pp. 91-154.

[9]Walter C. Till, *Die gnostischen Schriften des koptischen Papyrus Berolinensis 8502 (Texte und Untersuchungen,* 60) (Berlin, 1955). Cf. *infra,* ch. V.

B. CATALOG OF CODICES AND TREATISES

Codex I (Doresse No. XIII, Puech No. II) — The Jung Codex
about 168 pages (twenty-three pages are in the lot in Cairo
Museum)

1. *The Apocalypse of James* (differing from those in Codex V
2. *The Gospel of Truth* (*Evangelium Veritatis*)
3. *Discourse of Rheginos about the Resurrection*
4. *Treatise Concerning the Three Natures*
5. *Prayers of the Apostle Peter*

Codex II (Doresse No. X, Puech No. III) — 175 pages

6. *The Apocryphon of John* (a longer text, variant from that in
Codex III, quite close to that in Codex IV)
7. *The Gospel of Thomas*
8. *The Gospel of Philip*
9. *The Hypostasis* (*Essence*) *of the Archons* (*The Book of
Norea?*)
10. Untitled Revelation devoted to Pistis-Sophia
11. *The Exegesis* (?) *about the Being,* or *Exegesis of the Soul*
12. *The Book of Thomas the Athlete*

Codex III (Doresse No. I, Puech No. I) — about 134 pages and
fragments

13. *The Apocryphon of John* (a version closer to that in *BG*
than to that in Codex II) (this is listed as C 1 in Till's *BG.*)
14. *The Sacred Book of the Great Invisible Spirit* (*The Gospel
to the Egyptians?*)
15. *The Epistle of Eugnostos*
16. *The Wisdom of Jesus* (also found in *BG.*)
17. *The Dialogue of the Saviour*

Codex IV (Doresse No. II, Puech No. VIII)

18. *The Apocryphon of John*
19. *The Sacred Book of the Great Invisible Spirit* (same work
as in Codex III)

Codex V (Doresse No. III, Puech No. VII) — about 88 pages

20. *The Epistle of Eugnostos* (same as in Codex III)
21. *The Apocalypse of Paul*
22. *The Apocalypse of James*
23. *The* (*Second*) *Apocalypse of James* (not the same as No.
22)
24. *The Apocalypse of Adam to His Son Seth*

Codex VI (Doresse No. VI, Puech No. XI) — about 80 pages

25. *The Acts of Peter*
26. *Authentic Discourse of Hermes with His Son Tat*
27. *Thoughts of the Great Power*
28. Hermetic work without title
29. Sethian revelation with title missing
30. Hermetic treatise without title
31. Hermetic treatise nearly identical with paragraphs 21-29 of the Latin *Asclepius*

Codex VII (Doresse No. VII, Puech No. V) — 126 pages

32. *Paraphrase of Shem (Second Treatise of the Great Seth)*
33. *Apocalypse of Peter*
34. *The Teaching of Sylvanus*
35. *Revelation of Dositheus*

Codex VIII (Doresse No. IV, Puech No. IX) — 140 pages

36. A Revelation with missing title
37. *Discourse of Truth of Zoroaster, God of Truth*
38. *Epistle of Peter to Philip*

Codex IX (Doresse No. V, Puech No. X)

39. Titleless revelation attributed to the Great Seth
40. An Epistle about the Father of the All and the Primordial Adam
41. A Treatise in epistolary form
42. A titleless treatise against the scribes and Pharisees about the baptism of John and the water of Jordan and Jesus

Codex X (Doresse No. XII, Puech No. XII) — about 20 pages

42. Fragments of a mystical treatise about the cosmos

Codex XI (Doresse No. VIII, Puech No. VI)

44. *The Interpretation of Gnosis*
45. *The Allogenes Supreme (The All-Highest Strangers)*
46. *Revelation of Messos*

Codex XII (Doresse No. XI, Puech No. XIII)

47. Fragments of a work not yet fully identified

Codex XIII (Doresse No. IX, Puech No. IV)

48. *The Triple Discourse of the Triple Protennoia*
49. Revelation in epistolary form of Sethian origin (cf. No. 10)

It should be noted that those who have examined the manuscripts firsthand differ in their enumeration of individual works — now dividing, now combining items listed above. Until the full publication of the titleless and fragmentary works, the inventory can only be regarded as approximately correct. A recent listing divides item No. 32 above, giving the title in parentheses as a separate item, also adding another title, *The Thunder: Perfect Mind*, after item No. 25, and otherwise combines and adds titles to come out with a total of fifty-one treatises.

C. From Darkness to Light

Having tabulated the contents of the codices, we can now turn to a brief consideration of how these texts found their way from the double darkness of confinement within a jar in a cave to the light of the scholars' desks where they are now being studied, and to the full blaze of popular publication where the average man can read for himself the thoughts and ideas of a half-forgotten religion that threatened to overwhelm Christianity in the second and third centuries. While particulars of separate treatises will be reserved for the chapters dealing with them, the following résumé of how the findings became public will help in understanding why it has taken so long for these manuscripts — discovered before the Dead Sea Scrolls — to come to the attention of the world at large.

It would seem that the first report published was by H.-Ch. Puech and his pupil, Jean Doresse, who were in Egypt at the behest of the French Service of Antiquities.[10] About the same time Toga Mina also published an account of the find.[11] In this article the identification of the contents of Codex III, which had been acquired by the Coptic Museum, was made in part. Doresse saw that it partially paralleled the content of Berlin Codex 8502.[12] The report also included a description of Codex I, the Jung Codex.

Meanwhile, the other eleven codices had disappeared and reappeared, until finally in 1949 they were made available to the Coptic Museum for the purpose of having an expert evaluation made. The reports of their contents were soon forthcoming in various articles, most of them (unfortunately for the American

---

[10]"Nouveaux Écrits Gnostiques découverts en Égypte," *Compte rendus de l'Académie des Inscriptions et Belles-Lettres,* Feb. 20, 1948, pp. 87-95.
[11]"Le papyrus gnostique du Musée Copte," *V.C.,* II (1948), pp. 129-136.
[12]Till, *op. cit.*

reader) in little-known periodicals and in the French language.[13] Soon the find became known in America through two articles: the first, by Doresse, was published in 1950; the second, by Victor Roland Gold of Hamma Divinity School, appeared in 1952.[14]

While negotiations were going on for the purchase of the eleven codices by the Coptic Museum from Mlle. Dattari, Codex I had disappeared, and its original owner had died. Surreptitious offers of it were made to the Bollingen Foundation in New York, and to Dr. Gilles Quispel in Holland. The full story will be told in the chapter dealing with that codex. After the first flurry of articles in 1949-1950, very little additional information about the Chenoboskion documents appeared until the Jung Institute acquired Codex I.

The next big step forward was the publication in 1956 of *Coptic Gnostic Papyri in the Coptic Museum at Old Cairo, Vol. I,* under the direction of Dr. Pahor Labib, director of the Museum. Now, for the first time, the actual Coptic texts of part of Codex II, plus some pages missing from Codex I, were available for scholars to study, translate, and interpret. At first attention was centered on the *Gospel of Thomas,* which was heralded as a "fifth" Gospel. In recent years scholars have been working on the other treatises in the volume, including the *Apocryphon of John,* the *Gospel of Philip,* the *Hypostasis of the Archons,* the four pages of the *Gospel of Truth,* and the untitled work dealing with Pistis Sophia.

In the same year that the Coptic Museum published the first volume of texts, the Jung Institute published a sumptuous text edition with translations in French, German, and English, of the *Gospel of Truth* from Codex I.[15] Grobel presented his translation of the *Gospel of Truth* in 1960.[16] Meanwhile, the Suez crisis intervened and delayed further publication of the texts.

---

[13]Jean Doresse and Toga Mina, "Nouveaux Textes Gnostiques Coptes découverts en Haute-Égypte: La Bibliothèque de Chénoboskion," *V.C.,* III (1949), pp. 129-141. Cf. also Doresse's "Une bibliothèque gnostique copte découverts en Haute-Égypte," *Académie Royale de Belgique. Bulletin de la Classe des Lettres et des Sciences Morales et Politiques* 5, Serie XXV (1949), pp. 435-449, and "Une Bibliothèque Gnostique Copte," *La Nouvelle Clio,* I (1949), pp. 59-70.

[14]Doresse, "A Gnostic Library from Upper Egypt," *Archaeology,* III (1950), pp. 69-73; Victor Roland Gold, "The Gnostic Library of Chenoboskion," *B.A.,* XV (1952), pp. 70-88.

[15]Michael Malinine, Henri-Charles Puech, and Gilles Quispel, *Evangelium Veritatis* (Zurich: Rascher, 1956).

[16]Kendrick Grobel, *The Gospel of Truth: A Valentinian Meditation on the Gospel* (Nashville: Abingdon, 1960).

About 1959 a flood of scholarly articles and books dealing with the Chenoboskion texts began to appear. Most of these, naturally, have dealt with either the *Gospel of Truth* or the *Gospel of Thomas*. In the meantime, continental scholars, working from the Cairo photographic edition, had produced translations of the *Gospel of Thomas*, thus making it available to New Testament scholars not able to read Coptic.[17] Soon an "official" text edition, with a choice of translations in either German, French, or English, was published.[18] M. Doresse added an English translation of the *Gospel of Thomas* to the English version of his earlier French work dealing with the entire find.[19] The first American translation appeared in W. R. Schoedel's version.[20]

A translation of the *Hypostasis of the Archons* has appeared in German.[21] Meanwhile, the copy of the *Apocryphon of John* found in Codex Berolinensis 8502 was edited, translated into German, and published by Walter Till.[22] The present author prepared a text edition and translation of the *Apocryphon of John* from Codex II at the same time Soren Giversen was preparing his work based on that Codex and Codex III.[23] Also, several scholars have turned their attention to the *Gospel of Philip*. The chief English works dealing with that treatise are listed in the footnotes and bibliography to chapter 7. While several other treatises have been translated into German, the list above nearly exhausts those in English translation. More

---

[17]Johannes Leipoldt, "Eine neues Evangelium? Das koptische Thomasevangelium ubersetz und besprochen," *TLZ*, LXXXIII (1958), pp. 481-498; G. Garitte and L. Cerfaux, "Les paraboles du royaume dans l'Évangile de Thomas," *Le Muséon*, LXX (1957), pp. 307-327.

[18]A. Guillaumont, *et al., The Gospel According to Thomas* (New York: Harper & Bro., 1959).

[19]Jean Doresse, *Secret Books of the Egyptian Gnostics* (London, 1960); trans. of *L'Évangile selon Thomas ou Les paroles secrètes de Jésus* (Paris: Plon, 1958).

[20]In Robert M. Grant and David Noel Freedman, *The Secret Sayings of Jesus* (Garden City: Doubleday, 1960). A Swedish translation was made by Torgny Säve-Söderbergh, "Evangelium Veritatis och Thomas-evangeliet," *Symbolae Biblicae Upsaliensis*, XVI (1959), pp. 28-49. A Danish translation by Soren Giversen, *Thomas Evangeliet-Indledning, oversaettelse og kommentarer* (Copenhagen, 1959).

[21]Hans Martin Schenke, "Das Wesen der Archonten," *TLZ*, LXXXIII (1958), pp. 661-670, now included in his *Koptisch-gnostische Schriften aus den Papyrus-Codices von Nag-Hamadi* (jointly with J. Leipoldt), *Theologische Forschung* 20, Hamburg-Bergstedt: Reich, 1960.

[22]Cf. *supra*, note 9.

[23]Soren Giversen, *Apocryphon Johannis. Acta Theologica Danica* V (Copenhagen: Munksgaard, 1963). Cf. Andrew K. Helmbold, *The Apocryphon of John: A Text Edition, Translation, and Biblical and Religious Commentary*, Unpublished Ph.D. dissertation, Dropsie College, Philadelphia, 1961.

recent publications and projected publications containing English translations are noted in the pertinent chapters to follow.

D. WHAT MEAN THESE TOMES?

Some scholars evaluate this manuscript find as the greatest of the century; others rate it as equal in importance to the Dead Sea Scrolls. Some lines of thought regarding its importance can be pointed out, and the reader can keep them in mind as the various works are discussed. Then, at the end of the book, a summary of what we have already learned may set them in their proper perspective.

First of all, these volumes give us direct information about the beliefs of a vast movement in the second and third centuries which was so strong that it threatened to overwhelm or engulf the church, and to change Christianity into something other than the simple faith of the New Testament. This danger, and the reactions it brought about, can be seen in the perusal of the following chapter. The dangers that Gnosticism posed to Christianity did not cease at A.D. 500, but have continued (albeit in different forms) to the present day.

Secondly, some of the treatises profess to impart words of Jesus not contained in the canonical Gospels. Because the direct quotations from the words of Jesus in the Bible are relatively sparse, we are eager to find authentic words of Jesus that have not come down in the canonical Gospels. These *agrapha,* if such exist, will give us additional insight into the mind of Christ — and remember, Christians are to have the mind of Christ.

Thirdly, rationalistic "history of religion" scholars have sought to understand Christianity, or at least certain elements within it, as borrowings by the early church from pre-existent Gnosticism. A careful study of the Chenoboskion documents will show the truth or falsity of this position. Indeed, scholars have already pointed out the error of certain approaches along this line.

Fourthly, a careful study of the quotations from the Bible and references to the Bible in these texts will yield fruit of value to the technical scholar. Already (primarily from the *Gospel of Thomas,* but also from the other works) a wealth of material dealing with such matters as textual criticism, literary criticism, history of the canon, history of interpretation, etc., has accumulated.

Finally, although this list is not exhaustive, we can point out the value of studying these documents for an understanding of the philosophy and psychology of the Gnostics. Why did they believe what they believed? Why were they intrigued by a secret "gnosis"? Why did they reject salvation by faith in favor of salvation by mystic illumination? What aspects of their belief led some to asceticism, others to libertinism? How did this movement relate itself to similar groups such as the Mandaeans, the Hermetics, and the Manichaeans?

To evaluate these documents properly, one must have a brief insight into the Gnostic movement, its multiform manifestations, the reactions of the church to it, and how its "melody [or discord] lingers on." To these factors we now turn our attention.

SELECTED BIBLIOGRAPHY

Cross, F. L. (trans. and ed.). *The Jung Codex*. London: Mowbray, 1955.

Doresse, Jean. *The Secret Books of the Egyptian Gnostics*. London: Hollis and Carter, 1960 and New York: Viking Press, 1960.

——————. "A Gnostic Library," *Archaeology*, III (1950), pp. 69-73.

Gold, Victor R. "The Gnostic Library of Chenoboskion," *B.A.*, XV (1952), pp. 73-88.

Helmbold, Andrew K. "The Coptic Gnostic Texts from Nag Hammadi," *B.E.T.S.*, II (1959), pp. 15-19.

Nock, Arthur Darby. "A Coptic Library of Gnostic Writings," *J.T.S.*, n.s., IX (1958), pp. 314-324.

van Unnik, W. C. *Newly Discovered Gnostic Writings* (Studies in Biblical Theology No. 30). Naperville: Allenson, 1960.

Wilson, Robert McLachlan. "The Gnostic Library of Nag Hammadi," *S.J.Th.*, XII (1959), pp. 161-170.

II

THE HYDRA-HEADED HERESY

To understand and appreciate the individual works in the Nag Hammadi find, we must now turn to an over-all consideration of the religious movement called "Gnosticism."[1] Here we begin with the definitions of the term, consider the central ideas of the movement, the various sects within Gnosticism, the church's reaction to it, and medieval and modern manifestations and counterparts.

A. Definitions of Gnosticism

Many definitions of this term have been given. Perhaps the most famous is that of the German church historian, Adolph Harnack, who said: "Gnosticism is the acute Hellenization of Christianity" (*History of Dogma*, I, p. 226). The contents of the Nag Hammadi texts show that this definition is not accurate. More vivid and more exact is that of Dr. Walther that Gnosticism ". . . is a stealing of some Christian rags to cover heathen darkness."[2] A more recent student of the movement has defined Gnosticism as "The knowledge of the true nature of Divine things which seems to the initiate to light everything up and make everything clear."[3]

---

[1] The term here is used in its narrow, technical sense to mean those groups described in this chapter and the other closely related groups. The confusion of terminology that arises when some scholars speak of "Gnosis" and "Gnosticism" when they mean something vastly broader and more vaguely defined could be eliminated if other terms were used, or if (as is done in this work) the capital letters were reserved for the strictly Gnostic groups, and the lower case letters used to denominate the broader movement which included the Mandaeans, etc. Cf. Robert McL. Wilson, *The Gospel of Philip,* p. 16. This problem was discussed at the International Colloquium on the Origins of Gnosticism held at Messina, Italy, April 13-18, 1966. A tentative general agreement was reached which would reserve the term "Gnosticism" for the movements and groups fully developed in the second century. Cf. George W. MacRae, "Biblical News: Gnosis in Messina," *Catholic Biblical Quarterly,* XXVIII (1966), pp. 322-333.
[2] Cited by Louis Berkhof, *Reformed Dogmatics* (Grand Rapids: Eerdmans, 1937), p. 51.
[3] Francis C. Burkitt, *Church and Gnosis,* p. 6.

Actually, the term is a modern one, little used by the Gnostics themselves, and comes from the Greek root *ginosko,* meaning "to know." Literally, the Gnostics were the "knowers." They claimed their secret, esoteric knowledge was superior to that imparted through the revelation of God in Holy Scriptures. They said man was saved, not by faith, but by knowledge — not knowledge in general, but specific knowledge of the Gnostic myth, which was essentially self-knowledge. This is made clear as we turn to their own descriptions and definitions of Gnosticism.

Clement of Alexandria (*ca.* A.D. 200) quotes the Valentinian idea of Gnosticism in his *Excerpta ex Theodoto,* 78.2:

> But it is not only baptism which frees but also knowledge: knowledge of what we were, why we have come into being, where we were or at what point we have been inserted into the scheme of things, whither we are hastening, from what we are redeemed, what is being born, and what reborn.[4]

Irenaeus, Bishop of Lyons, described the Gnosticism of his day (*ca.* A.D. 180) in *Adversus Haeresies,* I.21.4:

> Perfect salvation is the cognition itself of the ineffable greatness: for since through "Ignorance" came about "Defect" and "Passion," the whole system springing from the ignorance is dissolved by knowledge. Therefore knowledge is salvation of the inner man; and it is not corporeal, for the body is corruptible; nor is it psychical for even the soul is a product of the defect and is as a lodging for the spirit: spiritual therefore must also be the form of salvation. Through knowledge, then, is saved the inner, spiritual man; so that to us suffices the knowledge of universal being: this is true salvation.

With this may be compared his statement in I.23.5, "By means of this *gnosis* [knowledge] a man receives power to overcome those very angels that made the world."

In the Gnostic *Book of Jeu,* I, ch. 1, this significant statement is made: "This is the book of the *gnoseis* [knowledge] of the invisible God, contained in the hidden mysteries which show the way to the elect generation."

Other definitions and examples could be multiplied, but enough has been said to show that the fundamental idea of Gnosticism was salvation by esoteric knowledge. This concept is worked out in various ways in the different sects within the movement, but is vital to them all.

---

[4] Cf. *E.V.* 22.3-15.

B. CENTRAL IDEAS OF GNOSTICISM

While the "salvation by knowledge" doctrine is the heart of the Gnostic theologies, it is not the only doctrine that sounded (and still sounds) strange to Christian ears. There were many other beliefs of the Gnostics that varied from orthodox Christian faith. Some were held by all Gnostic groups, some by only certain sects. Some were inextricably bound up with the "chief doctrine." Others were not essential to the Gnostic systems. To cover all the ramifications of the Gnostic theologies would be an impossible task, so here we must be content with pointing out some of the central ideas.

Basic to the Gnostic systems was a dualistic view of the world. The Persian dualism between light and darkness (cf. Gospel of John) was changed by the Gnostics into a dualism between spirit and matter: that is, between the world of sense and the world of pure being. Some "sparks" from the world of pure being have been imprisoned in the alien sphere of sense. Their redemption is accomplished by enlightenment, by *gnosis*. Just how and why the Gnostic came to believe that matter was evil is hard to understand in the twentieth century. Perhaps because he could not understand or control the forces of nature about and within him, he looked upon them as anti-god.

Along with his dualism, the Gnostic held that the Supreme Being was an Ineffable God, best described in terms of what He was not, rather than — for example, as the Westminster divines described Him — in positive terms. Some of the terms used to describe God and to stress His transcendence were "Father of All," "Unbegotten," "Ineffable," "The Unapproachable God," "The Abyss," "The Unknowable."[5] Hans Leitzmann says the Valentinian concept of the Ineffable God is expressed by a few telling words and symbols: "Above the universe dwells the prime Father who is also called Bythos and Chaos. He is invisible, incomprehensible, above time, and dwells unbegotten in eternal peace. . . ."[6] The Naasenes and the Barbelo-Gnostics called Him "The Man" or "The First Man," a designation common in Manichaean literature.

If an Ineffable God is to have contact with the world of sense, it must come about through a chain of intermediate

---

[5] Cf. *A.J.* 48.24-52.19, and also *E.V.* 17.7-9, 20.19-20. (Throughout this work *A.J.* is cited by page and line number from *CGP.*I, which reproduces the text of Codex II.)

[6] *The Beginnings of the Christian Church*, trans. Bertram Lee Wolf (New York: Charles Scribner's Sons, 1937), p. 387.

beings, each link in the chain, so to speak, being less divine and more earthy. So Gnosticism has as a prominent doctrine the idea of a series of emanations from the Highest God. These emanations in their totality are called the Pleroma (Greek "the fulness"). Usually they proceed from the High God in pairs. These pairs (syzygies) are often called Aeons (cf. *A.J.* 54.3). In most Gnostic systems the Pleroma totals thirty beings ranging from the Highest God at one end to Sophia at the other end. The best example of the Pleroma doctrine is taken from the Valentinian system. This is described by Irenaeus and by the author of the *Philosophumena*. The First Father or Supreme Being is characterized by divine transcendence and negative attributes best summed up as unfathomable profundity. His names, as well as those of most of the members of the Pleroma, are chosen to reflect the personification of divine attributes. Such personification, or more correctly, hypostatization, is seen already in the figure of wisdom in Proverbs and in the *Wisdom of Solomon,* and the treatment of "the Word" in the Gospel of John. Most of the terms are common, either in Greek philosophy, or in the Bible, or in both.

The Divine or Aeonic principle of pairs is somewhat unique, not at all to be compared to the marriages and unions of the gods in ancient mythologies. This uniqueness is demonstrated in the cultic "mystery of marriage" as set forth in the *Gospel of Philip*. After ages of contemplation of his own glory, the First Father, also called Abyss, takes as his consort Thought, also called Silence or Grace. The First Father wished to create the beginning of all things. This wish made his consort fecund, and she brought forth Mind, also called Monogenes (Only-begotten), who was the equal of his Father. Truth is produced to be the Aeon united with Mind. Mind and Truth produce Word and Life who, in turn, bring forth Man and Church. From Word and Life five further pairs emanate. From Man and Church six additional pairs proceed. These beings constitute fifteen pairs or thirty Aeons — the Pleroma. The farther away each Aeon is from the Father, the greater is its defect of the divine life, and the more intense is its desire for knowledge of the Father. However, only Mind (Nous) has the possibility of perfect knowledge of the Father. He becomes the agent of revelation. His preaching awakens the desire for God. The lowest of the Aeons, Sophia, is so full of passion to comprehend God that she falls and is placed outside the Pleroma.[7]

---

[7]*Ibid.,* pp. 388 ff.

Charlotte Baynes defines the Pleroma as follows:

Collectively, it represents the fullness of the divine perfections
and attributes, thus standing in sharp contrast, as a positive con-
ception, to the negative, ineffable aspect of the Deity of which
the human mind can form no definite notion.[8]

The last emanation, Sophia, was not content with her lot but
wanted to see the Father, who, according to Valentinian belief,
was invisible to the Aeons. As a result of her passion, Sophia
became fecund with a formless monster. When this monster
fell outside the Pleroma, it became the cause of the sensible
and material world. The monster of the Valentinians is the
equivalent of Yaldabaoth/Saclas/Samael of the Barbelo-Gnostics
and Sethians.

This brings us to a point where it is possible to understand
the Gnostic idea about the God of the Old Testament. Since
(according to Genesis) God created the world, for the Gnostic
that God must be the Demiurge, i.e., Yaldabaoth, not the transcendent head of the Pleroma. Since, according to the Gnostic,
matter is evil, only an inferior being could have created the
sensible world.

In this sensible world, man is created by the inferior God
according to some Gnostic system, or by angels according to
other systems. Within him is imprisoned a spark of the divine,
often called "a spark of light." This spark is described as being
in "ignorance," or "oblivion," or "forgetfulness," or "drunkenness."
All these terms picture the soul's condition as being unconscious
of its true nature and destiny. That which in Christianity is a
positive idea — sin as transgression — in Gnosticism is viewed as
a deprivation.

From this state man can be redeemed only by having the
ignorance removed, the oblivion or forgetfulness changed to
wakefulness and awareness, the drunkenness replaced by so-
briety. In other words, the Gnostic must come to himself, know
himself, and thus be redeemed. The Redeemer in most Gnostic
systems is the one who gives the revelation of knowledge
(gnosis) which arouses man and causes him properly to understand himself. This is plainly seen in the Apocryphon of John,
48.16–18; 71:30.

Closely connected with the doctrine of Redemption is the idea
of the ascent of the soul. In some Gnostic systems the planets
are viewed as seven heavenly warders who attempt to keep

---

[8]Charlotte H. Baynes, "A Coptic Gnostic Treatise," pp. 17-18 n., cited by
Ralph A. Marcus, "Pleroma and Fulfillment," V.C., VIII (1954), p. 202 n.

the soul from mounting up to bliss. The soul must overcome
these warders, or give the magic password whereby it is en-
abled to pass on to the next sphere. Some scholars have connected the ascent of the soul with Babylonian astral religion
antecedents. Others have traced it back to Egyptian conceptions. At any rate it contrasts with Christian redemption, which
is ethical, in that for the Gnostic the ascent is material, a trans-
plantation in space — if the soul can be said to occupy space.
It stresses the transition from the realm of sense to the realm of
pure being.

This introduces the Gnostic doctrine of Fate (Greek, *heimar-
mene*), which was thought of as above even the gods. The
whole of creation is subject to the planets (Archons or Cos-
mocrators), so that man is the subject of a veritable tyranny of
fate.[9] Other doctrines are more or less prominent in the various
schools of Gnosticism but these just discussed form the outstanding and distinctive elements of Gnosticism.

C. Sects within Gnosticism

If the early Corinthian church could quickly divide into vary-
ing groups that might be labeled "Paulicians, Simonians, Apollo-
sites, and Christians," likewise the Gnostics quickly proliferated
into many sects. Not always were they divisions from a central
group, but rather some came into existence in different places,
with different emphases, but out of the same syncretistic at-
mosphere with the combination of Iranian, Babylonian, Hebrew,
Christian, and Greek conceptions in the peculiar way which
makes the movement distinctive. Perhaps twenty-five or more
distinctive Gnostic groups could be listed. Here we are content to enumerate the more outstanding groups that seem to
have some relationship to the Nag Hammadi texts.

1. The Valentinians probably originated in Rome about A.D.
140. Their founder, Valentinus, had hoped to be named bishop
of Rome.[10] Whether his heretical ideas precluded that, or
whether his being denied a bishopric caused him to become
heretical is not settled. At any rate his brand of Gnosticism is
somewhat more philosophical, and perhaps even more closely
related to Christianity, than some of the so-called "Great Gnostics." He is credited with having written one of the important
texts in the Nag Hammadi library, the *Gospel of Truth.* His

[9]Origen's stress on free will may have been a reflex of this Gnostic doctrine.
[10]Cf. W. C. van Unnik, "The 'Gospel of Truth' and the New Testament," *The
Jung Codex,* ed. F. L. Cross, pp. 89-94, for a brief sketch of Valentinus.

ollower, Heracleon, wrote a famous *Letter to Flora,* which
tresses the similarities between Valentinianism and Christianity,
ut neglects to point out the distinctive heretical ideas of
Valentinianism. Marcus, another follower of Valentinus,
ounded the sect within Valentinianism called the Marcosians.

2. The Ophites (from Greek, *ophis,* a snake) and the closely
elated Naasenes (from Hebrew, *nahash,* a snake), as their
ames imply, were especially noted for their veneration of the
erpent. The chief outlines of their doctrines followed that of
he other Great Gnostics, but the serpent of Genesis 3 is given
a prominent part. In some systems the creator God, Yaldabaoth,
vas represented in art as a serpent. Among the Ophites the
ypical Gnostic Pleroma of Aeons was missing or undeveloped.

3. The Barbelo-Gnostics were known from their worship of the
emale being, Barbelo, who became the mother of Yaldabaoth,
he Demiurge.[11] In this system of doctrine Barbelo occupies
about the same position as the lower Sophia in Valentinianism.
The relationship of Barbelo-Gnostics to other "mother" cults
within Gnosticism (Simonianism, etc.) is not clear. However,
the evidence of the *Apocryphon of John* would point to a Syro-
Palestinian origin for Barbelo-Gnosticism.

4. The Sethians were, perhaps, the most numerous of the
many Gnostic sects. Their doctrines are quite close to those of
the Barbelo-Gnostics, with some important divergences. The
distinguishing characteristic of the group is the great stress put
upon Seth as the Redeemer, or Revealer of Gnostic secrets. It
is his seed, as in the Old Testament, that is the godly line.

In this enumeration we must omit such groups as the Simonians, the Marcionites, the Carpocratians, the Cerinthians, and
others not directly represented in the literature of Nag Hammadi thus far published. Likewise, groups related to, or out-
growths of, Gnosticism — such as the Mandaeans and the
Manichaeans — must be passed over. However, the Nag Hammadi texts show how closely intertwined these latter movements
are with basic Gnostic doctrines.

D.   REACTION OF THE CHURCH

Doctrines such as those advocated by the Gnostics could not
long pass unnoticed by the thinkers and leaders of the early
church. The first apologist of note was Justin, who lived and

---

[11] Cf. the Near Eastern Mother-goddess cults such as those of Ishtar, Isis, Atargates, Cybele, *et. al.*

wrote in Rome about A.D. 150. He was the teacher of Tatian, whose relationships with the Gnostics will be discussed under the *Gospel of Thomas*. His works included the now lost *Syntagma, Apologies,* and the *Dialogue with Trypho*. The most outstanding opponent of Gnosticism was Irenaeus, bishop of Lyons, France. About A.D. 180 he wrote his famous work, *Adversus Haereses,* dealing with the major Gnostic groups and their teachings. He had a firsthand knowledge of Valentinianism in Gaul. Evidently he had access to certain Gnostic texts, for his account of the Barbelo-Gnostics has a section which agrees almost word for word with the first half of the *Apocryphon of John*.

Another important apologist was Hippolytus. He was bishop of Rome and wrote his most famous work, *Refutations,* about A.D. 230. Epiphanius, bishop of Salamis on the island of Cyprus, wrote his all-inclusive *Panarion* (basket) about A.D. 375. In it he described each of the heretical groups as a particular species of serpent emerging from the basket. He told of having been enticed in Egypt by beautiful women who were using their charms to make converts to Gnosticism. He resisted their temptations and became, instead, a bitter opponent of Gnosticism.

Not only did the church produce literary figures whose pens fought the battle for purity of Christian doctrine, but it also came to develop several important distinctive features. If the germs of these features were already present in the first century, it was the Gnostic movement of the second century that hastened their development. These features included the definition of the canon, so that Gnostics could no longer claim their writings were Holy Scripture; the definition of the church so that the Gnostics could not claim that they were within the church (i.e., the church developed the theory of episcopal succession); and the definition of true Christian doctrine which gradually became formalized in the ecumenical creeds, but certainly was clearly defined earlier than the Nicene statement of A.D. 325.

E. MEDIEVAL AND MODERN MANIFESTATIONS

While the church triumphed over Gnosticism in the third and fourth centuries, the heresy did not completely disappear. The Great Gnostics were represented by the Audian sect of Mesopotamia in the seventh-eighth century. As indicated earlier, many Gnostic ideas were incorporated into Mandaeanism, which survives as a sect even today. These ideas were also

ken up by Mani in his Persian dualistic religion called Mani-
aeism, which spread over much of the civilized world in the
ird-fifth centuries. This doctrine went as far as Chinese
urkestan and won converts in all levels of society, including
ugustine who later became a great saint of the church. The
Manichees, in turn, survived in the middle ages in the Albi-
enses (Cathari) of southern France, and the Bogomils of
ussia.[12]

Today, aside from the Mandaeans, no gnostic sect survives.
However, many of the Gnostic beliefs still persist. Among
ese are the stress on the unknowability of the Supreme Being
cf. "God is totally other"), the allegorization or mythologization
f Scripture to fit the doctrines of Gnosticism (cf. current at-
mpts at re-interpreting the Scripture to avoid historical-gram-
atical interpretations), the belief that only the pneumatic part
f man is redeemable (cf. modern disavowals of a bodily resur-
ection), de-emphasis of eschatology in favor of the existential
oment. In fact, the silence of the *Gospel of Thomas,* for
xample, about sin, miracles, demons, etc. can be closely paral-
led in modern Christian theologies.[13] The esoteric language of
he Gnostics finds twentieth-century counterparts in the writings
f the philosophical theologians. The stress on self-knowledge
ather than ethics or doctrine reminds one of modern move-
ents not only in theology but also in psychology and psychiatry.
t is not accidental that Carl Jung, for example, is intensely in-
erested in Gnosticism. In view of the persistence of gnostic
deas in the twentieth century, we should have considerable
nterest in the Nag Hammadi texts.

SELECTED BIBLIOGRAPHY

Burkitt, Frances Crowfoot. *Church and Gnosis.* Cambridge: University Press, 1932.

Grant, Robert M. *Gnosticism and Early Christianity.* New York:
Harper and Bro., 1959.

onas, Hans. *The Gnostic Religion.* Boston: Beacon Press, 1963.

Wilson, Robert McLachlan. *The Gnostic Problem.* London: Mowbray,
1958.

---

[2]Cf. Robert M. Grant and David Noel Freeman, *The Secret Sayings of Jesus*
(Garden City: Doubleday, 1960), p. 78.
[3]*Ibid.,* p. 101.

III

THE JUNG CODEX (CODEX I)

Most intriguing is the story of the Jung Codex, officially listed as Codex I.[1] Evidently it was sold by the peasants who found it to Albert Eid, a dealer in Egyptian antiquities. Somehow it was spirited out of the country and offered for sale to a number of interested parties, including the Bollingen Foundation of New York, and also, according to the dealer, the University of Michigan. Finally, it was offered to Professor Quispel of the University of Utrecht. Then the death of the dealer added to the complications. With the help of Prof. C. G. Jung, the famous psychologist, Quispel tried (unsuccessfully) to persuade the Bollingen Foundation to acquire the manuscript. Through the intervention of Prof. C. A. Meier of Zurich, Mr. George Page of Wallisellen generously purchased the Codex on May 10, 1952, for presentation to the Jung Institute. Dr. Quispel, who had conducted the negotiations, was then able to proceed with a study of the Codex, although its purchase could not be made public until eighteen months later. No price is mentioned by Quispel (in his article in *The Jung Codex*), but the original owner had asked the Bollingen Foundation for $12,000. It is reported that as the various manuscripts of the Codex are edited and published, the originals are being returned to the Coptic Museum. Thus the entire collection, except those pages destroyed by the peasants, will repose at Cairo, preserving intact the Gnostic library. Frequently finds of this kind are parceled out among a number of museums and libraries, so it is gratifying to have this find collected in one place.

Not only is the history of the Jung Codex different, but its format, its language, and its provenance vary from the bulk of the Nag Hammadi find. The Codex is somewhat narrower and longer than most of the other codices. Its language is the Sub-

---

[1] The story is recounted by Quispel in *The Jung Codex*, pp. 40-44.

Nag Hammadi Gnostic Codices. This photograph indicates how the volumes looked when first acquired by the Coptic Museum. Since then work has proceeded on separating the pages and preserving them permanently under Plexiglas. The pages to the left are the missing pages of the GOSPEL OF TRUTH.

Achmimic dialect, which was probably common in the general area in which the codices were found. Finally, its content seems to come, mostly, from that circle of Gnostics called Valentinians.

Thirty-eight pages of the original codex became detached and were sold to the Coptic Museum.[2] Of these about thirty-four have been published in the photographic edition.[3] The Codex seems to have contained 136 pages, practically all of which are now identified, although some are very fragmentary. The catalog of treatises and pagination follows:

1. *The Apocryphon of James,* pp. 1-16.30

2. *The Gospel of Truth,* pp. 16.31-43.24. (Pp. 33-36 are at Cairo and are published in *CGP*.I.) This work will be discussed in detail in ch. 4.

3. *The Epistle of Rheginos,* sometimes called the *Discourse on*

Martin Krause and Pahor Labib, *Die Drei Versionen des Apokryphon des Johannes* (Wiesbaden: Harrassowitz, 1962), p. 38 f.
Pahor Labib, *CGP.I* (Cairo: Government Press, 1956). Cf. Krause and Labib, *ibid.,* p. 39, for complete identification of various fragments and pages.

the Resurrection, pp. 43.25-50.18. (Two pp., 48 and 49, are a
Cairo and appear as plates 1 and 2 of *CGP.* I)

4. *Treatise on the Three Natures,* pp. 51-134. All pages are a
Zurich except pp. 59-90, which are probably at Cairo. P[
65-82, 87-90 have been published in *CGP.*I.

5. *The Prayers of the Apostles,* pp. 135-136

Scholars who have studied these treatises feel that, with th
exception of the first work, they are definitely Valentinian. Fur
thermore, they are believed to have come from the primitiv
period of Valentinianism. Perhaps · Heracleon, the disciple c
Valentinus, was the author of the *Treatise on the Three Nature:*
while the master himself may have written the *Epistle c
Rheginos.* With this brief background, the individual texts ma
now be discussed.

A.   THE APOCRYPHON OF JAMES

This work is sometimes called the *Epistle of James* or th
Apocalypse of James. The former title seems preferable, for th
work opens with the usual Greek epistolary style (cf. Paul
letters). This controverts its claim to have been written in He
brew (i.e., probably Aramaic) characters. It purports to be
secret revelation given by Christ to James and Peter 550 day
after the resurrection. This period approximates that posited fc
Christ's post-resurrection appearances by the Valentinians an
Ophites as reported by Irenaeus (*Adv. Haer.* I.1.5. and I.28.
Harvey) and the 545 days mentioned in the *Ascension c
Isaiah,* 9.16, in a passage regarded as a Christian interpolatio
Van Unnik points out that some Gnostics believed there was
period of eighteen months (i.e., 540-550 days) between th
resurrection and the ascension.[4]

Here James is identified with the brother of the Lord, bu
also as the disciple, a feature to be discussed in chapter nine
This James was evidently held in high repute in certain Gnosti
circles. While some regarded Thomas, Philip, and Matthias a
the Gnostic inner circle, some other Gnostics gave a large plac
to Peter and James. The Valentinians themselves showed ho
they regarded John by the extensive use they made of hi
Gospel.

---

[4]*The Jung Codex,* pp. 83 f. The *Letter of James,* including plates, transcri
tions, and translations into French, German, and English, by M. Malinin
et. al. is to appear in 1967 (Zurich: Rascher Verlag).

As in some other Gnostic works, James is instructed to keep the revelation a secret, and to share it with only a chosen few. The work itself gives no clues as to the time or place of origin or authorship. There is no mention of it by title, nor any quotation from it in the Church Fathers. Its allusion to another epistle written six months earlier may refer to one of the Apocalypses of Codex V.

Turning now to the content, we find the work composed of sayings of Jesus occasioned (as in the *Gospel of Thomas*) by questions and statements of His disciples. Since the work is still unpublished, one can have only glimpses of its subject matter. It contains no typical Gnostic speculations about cosmogony, the cosmic drama, or the creation of man. Concerning questions about persecutions it declares they are willed by God and should be gladly accepted. However, the central motif seems to be "onward and upward" — a call to its readers to aspire heavenward. The Christian doctrine of redemption through Christ is here with emphasis upon the cross, but no elaboration of details. However, there does seem to be some stress placed on the typical Gnostic motif of knowledge (*gnosis*) as the key to eternal life. It is the revelation of Jesus which one must know. The *Epistle* avoids the Gnostic error of Docetism found in some Gnostic sects. As in other Gnostic works, true eschatology is lacking. The kingdom of God is future; however, it is not a chronological but an ethical event. Because of these variations from the Gnostic mainstream, or rather lack of clearly Gnostic motifs, van Unnik has labeled this work simply "vague, unreflecting Christianity." Evidently it was vague enough to warrant its inclusion in the Nag Hammadi "library," which otherwise is completely lacking in definitely orthodox texts. Puech regards it as Valentinian.[5]

The work answers the question, "Who is a true prophet?" by stating that prophecy, finding its head in John the Baptist, lost its existence when he lost his head. The work closes with an ecstatic ascension scene that has much in common with Jewish apocalypses. Since its author appears to know nothing of the Book of Acts or of Palestinian Christianity, it would seem that the work was produced in an out-of-the-way place. Egypt has been suggested. However, arguments from silence are always perilous. One can safely say only that it was probably produced in the first half of the second century by an unknown author at an unknown place.

Henri-Charles Puech, in Hennecke-Schneemelcher, *N.T. Apoc.*, Vol. I, p. 338.

B. The Epistle of Rheginos

This work has been published by the Jung Institute.[6] It was unknown, even by name, before the Nag Hammadi discovery. It contains, as the colophon indicates, a treatise on the resurrection. Here Valentinianism seems to deviate from the typical Gnostic belief which denied any kind of resurrection and believed in the ascent of the spirit to the Pleroma. Yet this *Epistle* is not quite orthodox Christianity for it held to a spiritual resurrection. Evidently I Corinthians 15 had not satisfactorily answered this question for the Gnostics, just as today some people cannot accept a "bodily" resurrection, but can believe in a vague "spiritual" resurrection. It seems quite probable that this work came from the pen of Valentinus himself. This would make a date before A.D. 150 seem most likely.

C. The Treatise on the Three Natures

Due to similarity of ideas, this work has been attributed to Heracleon, the leader of the Italian school of Valentinianism. He is better known as the first author of a Bible commentary because his work on John's Gospel deserves that honor. If his authorship is accepted, then the *Treatise* probably dates from *ca.* A.D. 150-160.

---

[6]Michel Malinine, *et. al., De Resurrectione* (Zurich: Rascher, 1963). (This work was unavailable to the author for use in this publication.)

Jean Doresse and Togo Mina Studying the First Manuscript Acquired by the Coptic Museum. This photo was taken in October, 1947.

Like the *Gospel of Truth* in the Jung Codex and the *Apocryphon of John,* this work contains elaborate speculations about the negative attributes of God. Yet this Being is not impersonal, but is intensely personal.[7] In his cosmogony, Heracleon (presuming he is the author) says the lower world has been made as an image of the higher world. He gives an allegorical explanation of Genesis 1-3. This preoccupation with creation and the opening chapters of Genesis is typically Gnostic, occasioned by their problem of reconciling the existence of an evil world with a good God.

The *Treatise* divides human history into three stages: (1) the hylic or Greek stage, (2) the psychic or Hebrew stage, (3) the pneumatic or Christian stage.[8] However, here the Valentinians seem to deviate from the "Great Gnostics" who frequently divided mankind into three groups: (1) the hylic or the un-redeemed, (2) the psychic or ordinary Christians, saved by faith, (3) the pneumatic or Gnostics, saved by knowledge. Most Gnostics felt that the hylic were doomed, while the other two classes found eternal bliss.

Patently, the *Treatise* rejects Greek philosophy, thus showing how Harnack erred, at least as far as the Valentinians were concerned. It does show some appreciation for Old Testament religion as the antecedent of Christianity. However, its lack of clear-cut distinctions between Christians and Gnostics would argue for an early date when the Gnostics regarded themselves as true Christians if not more exclusively as *the* true Christians.

SELECTED BIBLIOGRAPHY

Puech, Henri-Charles. In *New Testament Apocrypha,* Vol. I, ed. by Hennecke and Schneemelcher. Philadelphia: Westminster, 1963.
van Unnik, W. C. "The Origin of the Recently Discovered 'Apocryphon Jacobi,'" V.C., X (1956), pp. 149-156.

---

[7] Cf. the citation from it on p. 58, *The Jung Codex.*
[8] Here one is reminded of Compte's modern attempt at some such progressive pattern as well as Harvey Cox's more recent thesis in *The Secular City.*

IV

THE GOSPEL OF TRUTH

For a number of reasons the *Gospel of Truth* deserves separate treatment from the other works found in the Jung Codex. It was the first of the Nag Hammadi texts to be edited and translated, and was hailed by the popular press with exorbitant claims that it was a "fifth gospel."[1] Its content was known to Irenaeus about A.D. 180, thus indicating a very early date for its composition. He says concerning it:

> For the Valentinians, again, outstep all bounds of reverence in producing their own writings, and boast that they possess more Gospels than there really are. Indeed they have advanced to such a pitch of audacity that they give the title "Gospel of Truth" to a work composed by them not long ago, which agrees in no respect with the Gospels of the apostles, so that among them not even the Gospel is without blasphemy. For if what they produce is the "Gospel of Truth," yet is different from those handed down to us by the apostles, then any who will may learn (as is manifest from the writings themselves) that what has been handed down by the apostles is not the "Gospel of Truth."[2]

Its doctrines indicate that it was written when it was difficult to distinguish between orthodox Christianity and the emerging Gnostic heresy, thereby giving its readers an insight into the development of Gnosticism.

This "Gospel" names no author, which is unusual when one recalls the *Gospel of Thomas* and the *Gospel of Philip*. Scholars who have worked on the document feel that the author was probably Valentinus, an aspirant for the bishopric of Rome *ca.*

---

[1]Michel Malinine, Henri-Charles Puech, Gilles Quispel, *E.V.* (Coptic text with German, French, and English translations) (Zurich, 1956).

[2]Irenaeus, *Adv. Haer.* III.11.9 (Harvey), cited by Henri-Charles Puech, "The Gospel of Truth," in *N.T. Apoc.,* I, ed. Edgar Hennecke, Wilhelm Schneemelcher, and Robert McL. Wilson (Philadelphia: Westminster, 1963), p. 233, and by Gilles Quispel, "The Jung Codex and Its Significance," in *The Jung Codex,* ed. F. L. Cross (London, 1955), p. 48.

A Page from the GOSPEL OF TRUTH (F. IX, p. 17 of EVANGELIUM VERITATIS).

A.D. 140, who later became known as a heretic and the founder of the Gnostic school called Valentinianism.[3] The lack of either an introduction or a colophon to indicate the author and the addressees is not unique in Gnostic texts, but it is unusual. Perhaps the explanation of this omission is to be found in the nature of the work, a topic that will be discussed shortly. The modern title is taken from its opening words. Contrary to frequent Gnostic practice (but not among the Valentinians, which is significant), there is no invocation or use of ancient prophet or apostolic figure to lend authority to the work as in Sethian or Barbelo-Gnostic works.

Because of the primitiveness of the content, scholars have dated this work from the very early stages of Valentinianism. Quispel and van Unnik think it may come from as early as A.D. 140-145.[4] It shows no traces of the developed Valentinianism, which, after the time of Valentinus, split into several divisions such as the Marcosians, etc. The treatise is evidently a translation of a Greek original. In addition to its citation by Irenaeus, there is some evidence that it was known in the third century by Origen (*Hom. on Luke* 24[5]), and also by Pseudo-Tertullian (*Adv. Omnes Haer.* 4, p. 221, 9-13, Kroymann), and perhaps by Tertullian (*de praescr. Haer.* 25, p. 30, 15-31, Kroymann).

A. THE NATURE OF THE WORK

The English title and its Latin counterpart, *Evangelium Veritatis*, are taken from the opening words of this work. Irenaeus used this title. However, some modern scholars look upon this expression as simply a cry of joy by one who has received its good news. If this be true, then the phrase indicates its essential nature rather than its technical name. When it is recalled that the word "gospel" (good news, *evangelism*, *evangellos*) had not come to mean in the middle of the second century what it means today — an account of the life, teachings, deeds, death,

---

[3]Cf. Gilles Quispel, *ibid.*, p. 50, W. C. van Unnik, "The 'Gospel of Truth' and the New Testament," in *The Jung Codex*, ed. F. L. Cross (London, 1955), pp. 99, 103 f., and the same author in *Newly Discovered Gnostic Writings* (*Studies in Biblical Theology* No. 30) (Naperville: Allenson, 1960), p. 63. The same opinion is held by the editors of the text, *E.V.*, p. xiv; by Arthur Darby Nock, "A Coptic Library of Gnostic Writings," *J.T.S.*, IX (1958), p. 323; by Hans Jonas, "Evangelium Veritatis . . ," *Gnomon*, XXXII (1960), and others.

[4]*Jung Codex*, pp. 54, 97-104; cf. *Newly Discovered Gnostic Writings*, pp. 61 ff.

[5]Puech, *N.T. Apoc.*, I, pp. 233 f.; cf. van Unnik, *Jung Codex*, p. 89 n.

and resurrection of Christ — but rather that it meant "good news," then this view seems correct.

This treatise presents the revelation of the Truth, that is Truth as the Gnostic understood it, or perhaps as it was understood by a writer well on his way to becoming a Gnostic. This truth is concerned with man's lot, man's need of redemption, and how that redemption is to be effected. On that basis it is "good news," the "Gospel." Therefore, the work is a discourse, or meditation, or homily on the meaning of this Truth, this message that the Gnostic wishes to impart as his "good news" to the world. It is concerned with "the redemption of them who knew not the Father" (Pl. 16 f.).

The content will be discussed more specifically in the next section of this chapter. Suffice it here to say that the meditation shows the necessity of redemption (cf. Romans 1:18–3:20), and the mode of appropriating that redemption. The necessity is found in the ignorance of the Father (which is really the "original sin" for the Gnostic). This ignorance is corrected by the appearance of Jesus who gives men the knowledge of the Father.[6] Doresse hints that the *Gospel of Truth* may be a meditation — albeit, a very abstract one — "upon a myth which is never imparted to us in its own terms, but which, judging by certain details, must have been a cosmogony analogous to those disclosed in other Gnostic treatises."[7] This theory raises two questions. The first of these is a question of extensive ramifications for the history of Gnosticism and the dating of various Gnostic texts, especially those from Nag Hammadi thus far published. It is the "chicken or the egg" question: which came first — mythological or philosophical gnosis? The second question is whether or not the *Gospel of Truth* (like the later Valentinian work by Ptolemaeus, a disciple of the master, entitled *Epistle to Flora*) deliberately disguises, "soft pedals," and otherwise hides the true nature of Valentinianism so that the readers will think it is orthodox Christianity and unthinkingly accept it. Modern counterparts on the theological scene are not difficult to find, wherein theologians use the old words of orthodox Christianity, but, like weasels in the hen-house, suck the words dry of their original meanings and present an empty shell as if it were the genuine article.

---

[6]Cf. Puech, *ibid.*, pp. 239 f. for details.
[7]Jean Doresse, *Secret Books of the Egyptian Gnostics* (London, 1960), p. 240.

B. The Doctrine Expounded

An analysis of the teaching or theology of the *Gospel of Truth* might well start with an examination of what it does not contain. Here some comparisons are worth making. First of all, in contrast to Christianity, the treatise does not give an orderly account of the life and work of Jesus. While it does give a few biographical glimpses in introducing some of its teaching,[8] by and large it is not interested in Jesus as a historical figure. However, it is Christocentric, whereas most Gnostic documents are not. In contrast to the books of the New Testament, it is not rooted in the Old Testament, a feature it shares with many Gnostic documents (cf. Marcion's rejection of the Old Testament, and the reworking of the Hebrew Scriptures in the *Apocryphon of John*).

The *Gospel of Truth* lacks distinctive Christian doctrines in the realms of eschatology, ethics, and hamartiology. Instead of speaking of "sin," *E.V.* mentions only ignorance and error. Salvation by Gnosis is a psychological experience, real or imaginary, described as follows:

> . . . man is re-established in himself, again remembers himself, and becomes conscious of himself, of what he really is by nature and origin. In this way he knows or reknows himself in God, knows God, and becomes conscious of himself as an effluence from God and a stranger in the world. He thus acquires, with the possession of his "ego" and his true and ontological being, the meaning of his destiny and the final certainty of his salvation, thus discovering himself as a being who, by right and for all eternity is saved.[9]

This is just the reverse of Christianity. When the prodigal son (who is symbolic of all men) comes to himself, he discovers that he is estranged from the Father, and finds that his real self is a sinful self. Christian salvation might be classed as a psychological experience, but it is rooted in historical facts rather than in philosophical speculation. The Gnostic (and modern) concept of salvation by having one's eyes opened and becoming like the Deity is as old as the Garden of Eden.

Secondly, if the *Gospel of Truth* deviates from orthodox Christian doctrine, it also falls far short of typically Gnostic — or even full-blown Valentinian — doctrine. As noted above, this is one reason the document has been dated very early. Missing from

---

[8]Puech, *op. cit.*, pp. 237 f. gives representative examples.

[9]Puech, "The Jung Codex and the other Gnostic Documents," in *The Jung Codex*, ed. F. L. Cross (London, 1955), p. 29.

the *Gospel of Truth* is the typical speculation about Aeons. These Aeons are usually developed in a scheme of thirty beings of fifteen pairs. In this chain of beings, each one is a little less divine and a little more material. The last of these in most Gnostic systems is Sophia (or the lesser Sophia), who yearns to make a creation and does so without a consort, thus producing the "Fall," or split within the Pleroma, and imprisoning something of the divine in material form through the activity of her offspring who becomes the Demiurge (called Yaldabaoth in some systems). This Demiurge is missing from the *Gospel of Truth*. Another typically Gnostic motif, the ascent of the soul to the heavens or to the Father, is missing or only faintly referred to. However, these arguments from silence cannot be given too much weight. Even if the really distinctive features of Valentinianism are missing, their absence can be explained on the basis of the nature of the treatise. One would not expect a Christian sermon on the "Joy of Salvation" to cover every Christian doctrine.

On the other hand, the *Gospel of Truth* does state many doctrines common to several schools of Gnosticism: (1) not-knowing, forgetfulness, oblivion of the Father as the real "original sin"; (2) Jesus is set forth as a Saviour, but a Saviour by *gnosis*, not by vicarious suffering; (3) man is saved by knowledge, for "whosoever has knowledge understands from whence he has come and whither he goes" (Pl. 22). Van Unnik thinks that the *Gospel of Truth* could be considered as an elaboration of Acts 17:25-30: "We live in God and know him not." Gnosis, then, gives the key for the understanding of the ultimate verities: "who we were, what we have become; where we were, whereinto we are cast; whither we are hastening, from what we are delivered; what generation (birth) is, and what regeneration (rebirth) is."[10] It is simply an attempt to get man to know and accept his true ontological situation, and thereby to be saved.[11]

C. Relations to the New Testament

As indicated above, Old Testament references or allusions in the *Gospel of Truth* are almost non-existent. However, this is not true of the New Testament. The work abounds in such citations, allusions, and echoes. It draws very heavily from the canonical Gospels, especially John. In contrast to Marcion's "meat axe" approach, it uses practically all the books of the New

---

[10]van Unnik, *Newly Discovered Gnostic Writings*, p. 22, citing Clement of Alexandria, *Excerpta ex Theodoto*, 878.2.

[11]van Unnik, *Jung Codex*, p. 106.

Testament in one way or another, indicating thereby that at this early date the author's New Testament was substantially identical with what was later decreed to be the official canon of the church.[12] This fact concerning Valentinus was supposedly pointed out already by Tertullian or Pseudo-Tertullian in the third century.

Along with other Gnostic treatises from other schools of Gnosticism, especially the *Gospel of Thomas* and the *Gospel of Philip*, the *Gospel of Truth* does not make literal citations of the canonical Gospels as do the apostolic fathers. Rather the New Testament materials are reworked and brought into the *Gospel of Truth* as echoes. The writer attaches new meanings to familiar New Testament passages. We shall return to a discussion of the Biblical materials in this Valentinian document in the final chapter of this volume to note their bearing on matters of Biblical criticism. It is sufficient for the present to note that Valentinus (or whoever wrote the treatise) was an eisegete, one who reads meanings into the Scripture, rather than an exegete, one who unfolds the meanings found in Scripture.

SELECTED BIBLIOGRAPHY

Giversen, Soren. "Evangelium Veritatis and the Epistle to the Hebrews," *Studia Theologica*, XIII (1959), pp. 87-96.

Grobel, Kendrick. *The Gospel of Truth: A Valentinian Meditation on the Gospel.* New York: Abingdon, 1960.

Isenberg, W. W. Translation of the *Gospel of Truth* in *Gnosticism: A Source Book of Heretical Writings*, ed. Robert M. Grant. New York: Harper and Bro., 1961.

Malinine, Michel, Henri-Charles Puech, and Gilles Quispel. *E.V.* (*Studien aus dem C. G. Jung Institut*, VI). Zurich, 1956. This volume did not include the missing pages that are at Cairo, but these pages were published as a *Supplementum* (Zurich and Stuttgart, 1961) by the same editors with the addition of Walter C. Till.

Puech, Henri-Charles. "The Gospel of Truth," in *N.T. Apoc.*, I, ed. Edgar Hennecke and Wilhelm Schneemelcher. Philadelphia: Westminster, 1963, pp. 233-241.

Wilson, Robert McLachlan. "The Gospel of Truth," appendix 2 to *N.T. Apoc.*, I, ed. Hennecke and Schneemelcher. Not a complete translation, but very long extracts of the work.

---

[12]The important church councils that handed down "official" canons were Laodicea, A.D. 364; Hippo, A.D. 393; Carthage, A.D. 397 and 419. For details consult R. Laird Harris, *Inspiration and Canonicity of the Bible* (Grand Rapids: Zondervan, 1957); Floyd V. Filson, *Which Books Belong in the Bible?* (Philadelphia: Westminster, 1957); William Barclay, *The Making of the Bible* (New York: Abingdon, 1961).

V

THE APOCRYPHON OF JOHN

Something of the popularity and the importance of this work can be judged by the fact that three copies of it were found at Nag Hammadi (in Codices II, III, and IV), while still another copy had been found fifty years earlier, but remained unpublished until after the Nag Hammadi find had been publicized. In 1896 Carl Schmidt announced the discovery of the *Apocryphon of John* in a codex that also contained the *Gospel of Mary* (Miriamme), the *Wisdom of Jesus Christ*, and the *Acts of Peter*.[1] Some of these works reappear in the Chenoboskion texts. Through a series of incredible misfortunes this manuscript did not see the light of printer's ink, although Schmidt had progressed as far as having it set in type only to have the type accidentally destroyed. After Schmidt's demise, the late Dr. Walter Till took up the task, which was disrupted by World War II and brought to completion only in 1955.[2]

The colophon at the end of the treatise attributes it to John. In the preamble to the body of the text he is called "the brother of James, these who are the sons of Zebedee." At the end of the revelation the Saviour instructs John to write down what had been revealed to him. As in the case of the Gospels of *Thomas* and *Philip*, so here we have the borrowing of an apostle's name to lend credence to the content of the work.

The text of *BG.* probably should be dated around A.D. 400 or a little later, while the text found in Codex II of the Nag Hammadi texts may date from about A.D. 340. However, the more important question is that of the date of the composition, since these texts so obviously are translations from Greek originals, and probably had been much copied. On the basis of the close

---

[1]C. Schmidt, "Ein vorirenaische gnostisches Originalwerk. . ," in *Sitzungsberichte des kgl. preussischen Akademie des Wissenschaft*, 1896, pp. 839-847.
[2]Walter C. Till, *Die gnostischen Schriften des koptischen Papyrus Berolinensis 8502 (Texte und Untersuchungen 60)* (Berlin, 1955).

Codex II, Half Opened.

similarity — even verbal agreement in places — of the *Apocryphon*
with Irenaeus' description of a Gnostic sect called the Barbelo-
Gnostics (*Adv. Haer.* I.29), Schmidt said that Irenaeus used
the *Apocryphon* in preparing his polemic.[3] On this basis some
have dated the writing of the *Apocryphon* before A.D. 180.
Others think Irenaeus and the *Apocryphon* used a common
source. The version in Codices II and IV mentions a *Book of
Zoroaster*. When more is known about this latter work, the
dating of the *Apocryphon* may become more definite. On the
other hand, some regard this passage in Codices II and IV as a
later interpolation.[4]

At the beginning of the work there is a confrontation of John
by a Pharisee, Arimanios, who accuses Jesus of misleading His
disciples and turning them away from the traditions of the
fathers. This would indicate a date after the break between

[3]C. Schmidt, "Irenaeus und seine Quelle in Adv. Haeres. I.29," *Philotesia, Paul
Kleinert zum LXX Geburtstag dargebracht,* 1907, pp. 315-316.
[4]Giversen, *Apocryphon Johannis,* pp. 280 ff., gives a full treatment to this and
related problems.

Judaism and early Christianity. If, as Quispel and others maintain, the Valentinians philosophized and Hellenized the earlier Gnostic myth,[5] then the *Apocryphon* may be as early as the first quarter of the second century A.D. This date is further confirmed by the use, in Codices II and IV, of the co-ordinate style, "and . . . and," in seeming imitation of the canonical Apocalypse of John. In the mid-second century doubt was cast on the authenticity of the Biblical Apocalypse, so it would seem reasonable to assume that the Gnostic work was written before that time. Additional evidence for an early date is found in the colophons of these two codices which conform to the format in the canonical Gospels.

Others think the *Apocryphon* mythologized the more philosophical Valentinian system which is presented, for example, in the *Gospel of Truth*. Since a date of *ca.* A.D. 140 for the *Gospel of Truth* seems well established, this approach would date the *Apocryphon* between A.D. 150-160. However, this does not seem to allow adequate time for the supposed process of mythologization. On the whole, the weight of evidence seems to favor an early second-century date for the original composition of the *Apocryphon.*

---

[5]Gilles Quispel, *Gnosis als Weltreligion,* p. 11, cited by Robert McL. Wilson, "Gnostic Origins," *V.C.,* IX (1955), p. 206. Cf. also H.-C. Puech, *The Jung Codex,* p. 26, and Walter C. Till, "Die Gnosis in Aegypten," *La Parole del Passuto,* XII (1949), p. 231 ff., cited by Wilson, "Gnostic Origins Again," *V.C.,* XI (1957), p. 108.

Codex II, Reverse Side.

There is some scholarly debate about the priority of texts. The text given in Codices II and IV is vastly different from that of *BG*. The Codex III version is close to *BG*., but quite frequently gives independent readings, or readings agreeing with Codices II and IV and disagreeing with *BG*. On the basis of the fact that Codices II and IV are longer, some have felt that they are later than *BG*. The main additions to this longer version are as follows: (1) the mixing of the Light with Darkness, 59.11 ff.; (2) the extended passage giving the names of the angels who created the various parts of the body, and the names of the *daimons* in charge of the various passions and related to various ills, 63.29 to 67.12; (3) the dialogue between Jesus and John about salvation, including the destiny of souls. However, there is some evidence that the version of *BG*. here had been misunderstood and hence mutilated and reworked by a copyist; (4) the descent of the Saviour into the Abyss to deliver the first man.

Added to these details is the fact that Irenaeus stops his account at the point where John begins his interrogation of the Saviour. (However, the dialogue style is introduced earlier when Jesus tells John the answers to his unuttered questions. The dialogue style is early — it is used in the *Gospel of Thomas*, *Wisdom of Jesus Christ*, and the *Apocryphon of James*.) Irenaeus' version does not agree with either of the two versions discussed. All in all, the question of priority must await further light.[6] It seems as likely that the longer version might have been abbreviated, as that the shorter version was amplified. It is true that the stress on magical names was at its height in the third and fourth centuries, but was not unknown in the second. The fact that all texts show evidences of errors in copying — some auditory, some visual — makes us proceed with caution.

The *Apocryphon* is concerned chiefly with answering ques-

---

[6]Cf. ref. to Giversen above for extensive discussion. Doresse, *The Secret Books*, p. 241 n., seems to feel that Codex II is later (cf. his *Les livres sécrets . . .*, p. 219). Puech, *Coptic Studies in Honor of Walter Ewing Crum*, p. 104, says Codex II is more ancient. Also dealing with the literary critical problems is an article not available to this writer: Hans MartinSchenke, *Nag Hamadi Studien* I, *Z. Relg. Geist.*, XIV (1962), pp. 57-63. Cf. also three articles by Rudolph Kasser: "Le 'Livre secret de Jean' dans ses differente formes textuelles coptes," *Museon*, LXXVII (1964), pp. 5-16; "Bibliothèque gnostiques I. Le Livre Secret de Jean= Apocryphon Ioannou," *Revue de Theologie et Philosophie*, XVII (1964), pp. 140-150; "Textes gnostiques: Remarques a propos des editions recentes du Livre Secret de Jean et des Apocalypses de Paul, Jacques et Adam," *Museon*, LXXVIII (1965), pp. 71-98.

ons about man's nature, but these questions bring up the
elated questions about man's release from the prison (the body)
n which he finds himself. The treatise purports to answer
questions such as: Why is man what he is? How is man to be
perfected? The central thrust is upon man's coming to know his
true nature, rather than upon a redemption offered to man.
While there is some teaching about salvation (brought by the
impartation of *gnosis,* true knowledge), and the coming age
(Aeon), yet the main thrust is not eschatological, but is upon
the mythological past and upon the existential moment when
man comes to understand himself and know the secret.

With this brief sketch as to the character of the work, we
now turn to a summary of its content. This summary is based
upon the longer versions of Codices II and IV but is indebted
to the other versions for clarifications at various points. Ex-
planatory matter by the present author is enclosed in parentheses. The summary is divided into seven major parts:

... THE PRELUDE — CHRIST'S APPEARANCE TO JOHN

As John was going up to the temple, a Pharisee, Arimanios,
accosted him and asked him where the Saviour had gone.
Arimanios said Jesus had led the disciples astray, and had
turned them from the traditions of the fathers. Whereupon John
was in grave doubt, so went to a mount (Olivet), presumably
to meditate and seek answers to the questions just raised. There
Jesus appeared to him in a scene replete with details taken from
Revelation 1. In the revelation He told John that He is the
Father, the Mother and the Son, a common Gnostic formula in
which there is probably a reminiscence of a Semitic background,
for in Hebrew (but not in Greek) the word "Spirit" is feminine.
He is the eternal One who is to reveal to John "what was, and
what is, and what shall be." This revelation John was to pass
on to his fellow disciples. This latter instruction is repeated at
the close of the work.

3. THE DESCRIPTION OF THE SUPREME ONE

Piling name upon name, adjective upon adjective, and negation upon negation, the *Apocryphon* proceeds to describe the
head of the Gnostic hierarchy of spiritual beings in terms of
His total transcendence. He is invisible and inconceivable —
totally ineffable. He is over all Aeons. He rests quietly in
silence. So transcendent is He that He cannot even be called
"God." (This description of God in negative terms is found

also in the *Gospel of Truth* and, to a limited extent, in the
Church Fathers.)

C.　The Creation of the Pleroma

As the Supreme One gazed at His own likeness in the Light
that surrounded Him, by His Thought (Ennoia), He created a
female being called Barbelo (possibly meaning "from Arbela,"
referring to Ishtar of Arbela). She is created in the image of her
father, and is an androgynous (male-female) being. At her
request four Aeons come into existence: Foreknowledge, Indestructibility, Eternal Life, and Truth. They, likewise, are androgynous, so with the Barbelo comprise the Aeonic Pentad/Decad.
Once more Barbelo begets, and produces Christ (Monogenes).
Christ, in turn, produces four Light Aeons: Harmozel, Oriel,
Daveithe, and Heleleth. Each of these has three Aeons ac-
companying it to make up a total of twelve Aeons. Wisdom
(Sophia) is the last of these. Now the Perfect Man (Pigera-
Adaman?) appears and is placed over the first Light-Aeon. Seth
is put over the second Light-Aeon. The seed of Seth is placed
over the third. The souls of the Holy Ones (otherwise not
identified) are placed over the fourth Aeon. Thus is completed the Gnostic Pleroma. (If the Barbelo is considered a
consort of the Supreme One, and if it is assumed that Christ,
Mind, Word and Will — previous emanations — are all androgynous, one arrives at the typical Gnostic total of thirty for the
complete Pleroma.)

D.　Wisdom's Fall and Yaldabaoth's Creation

Wisdom, the last of all the Aeons, wished to bring forth a
creation without the consent (union) of her partner. Her desire
brought forth a monster with a serpent (dragon) form with a
lion face. So no one would know her ignorance, she placed him
in a light-cloud. He is named Yaldabaoth (meaning, probably
Child of Chaos), also Samael and Saclas (names attested in
Jewish literature as epithets for Satan). This Yaldabaoth in the
Gnostic system is Jahweh of the Old Testament, the creator of
the material world and man as we know him. Taking some of
his Mother's power (i.e., the Divine essence), he created other
Aeons (by union with his ignorance?) in a flame of fire. He
made twelve powers (Archons): Athoth, Harmas, Kalila, Jabel,
Adonaiou, Cain, Abel, Abiresene, Jobel, Armoupiel, Melcher,
Adonein, and Belias. (Perhaps these are to be related to the
twelve signs of the Zodiac.) The first seven reign over the

eavens and the last five over the Abyss. Yaldabaoth continues
is creation with the twelve Archons each making seven powers,
nd each power making six angels until (with some details
acking) 365 angels are created. The Archons have heads of
arious animals, heavenly and non-heavenly names, and ab-
tract qualities such as Goodness, Forethought, etc. The non-
eavenly names are close to those previously listed: Athoth,
Cloaiou, Astaphois, Jao, Sabaoth, Adonin, Sabbade. These names
re given by Yaldabaoth to strengthen them. The heavenly
ames are given by the beings of the world above (i.e., the
Pleroma) so that thereby they can bring about the loss of power
nd the destruction of Yaldabaoth's cosmic entities. (This motif
of a second name by which a power can be controlled is well
attested in the *Testament of Solomon*.)

Upon seeing his creation, Yaldabaoth in pride cries out, "I
am a jealous god, and there is no other God except me" (cf.
Exod. 20:5; Isa. 45:5-6). The Gnostic author points out that by
his statement Yaldabaoth proves the existence of another god;
otherwise how could he be jealous? (At this point Irenaeus'
account ends and the first question of John is asked.) Wisdom
(Sophia), in her agitation at her monstrous offspring and his
impiety, is going to and fro. John asks what this means. The
Saviour replies that it is not to be understood as Genesis 1:2
(where the Spirit moves over the face of the Abyss). Wisdom
(Sophia) repents of her sin and is blessed by the higher powers,
i.e., the Pleroma, and is put in the Ennead until she is corrected
rom her fall. Her spouse comes to her to correct her defect.

E.   THE CREATION OF MAN

In response to Yaldabaoth's blasphemy, a voice comes from the
Aeonic Heaven, "The Man exists and the Son of Man." (This
expression is later clarified in the untitled work of Codex II.)
Then the Supreme One, the Perfect One, reveals his likeness
(i.e., the likeness of the first man). The foundations of the
Abyss move. Yaldabaoth's Aeon trembles all over. He cries to
his Archons, "Come, let us create a man according to the
image of God, and according to our likeness, so that his image
shall be to us for a light" (cf. Gen. 1:26). Each of the heavenly
powers makes an essence (bone, skin, etc.) of man according to
the likeness he had seen in the water. Yaldabaoth says, "Let us
call him, Adam."[7] Then the 365 angels make the parts of the

---

[7] Doresse, *Secret Books*, p. 205 n., points out that the seven bodily elements
fashioned by the seven planets is also a feature of Iranian religion and of
Manichaeanism.

body, and its passions (this list of angels and *daimons* is not in
the shorter version of *A.J.*). The Gnostic author says even
his list is not complete, but refers his readers to the *Book of
Zoroaster* (also found at Nag Hammadi) for a more complete
list.

This earthly Adam is lifeless and inert. By a stratagem he
is given life. When Wisdom (Sophia) asks the Supreme One for
permission to recover the Power she had imparted to Yaldabaoth,
the Supreme One sends down five lights in the form of Yaldabaoth's angels. They advise Yaldabaoth to breathe into Adam
some of his spirit, which he does. By this trick, Yaldabaoth is
deprived of power and Adam is given life. (In *BG.* it is God
who breathes life into the inert man.) Not only does Adam
receive life, but he becomes a shining being, superior to his
creators. They become jealous and cast him into the nether-
world of matter.

F. The Fall of Adam

The Supreme One, the Metropator, had compassion on the
power of Sophia now residing in Adam. Therefore, He sent
down a Thought of Light — Zoe (Life), to save Adam. Meanwhile, the Archons had taken fire, earth, water, and wind (the
four Greek primary elements), and had created a material body
for Adam (who until now had been only a psychic being).
This material body became a tomb for the refashioned man. This
body is called the "bond of forgetfulness." This man is mortal,
the first "split."

The Archons proceed to put Adam in Paradise and encourage
him to eat of the Tree of Life whose parts and characteristics
are all perverse and harmful. In the Tree of Knowledge is hidden
the Thought (Epinoia) of Light. John asked if the serpent had
taught Adam to eat. The Saviour replies that the serpent taught
Adam to partake of the desire for procreation (whereby more
souls would be created to come under the serpent's dominion).
However, the Thought of Light kept Adam from following the
serpent's advice.

Wishing to extract his Power from Adam, Yaldabaoth brought
a forgetfulness upon Adam. This power — the Thought of Light
— eluded Yaldabaoth when he opened Adam's side (cf. Gen. 2),
and he caught only part of it, from which he formed woman.
When Adam regained consciousness, he said, "This is now bone
of my bone, and flesh of my flesh. For this cause shall a man
leave his father and mother and cleave unto his wife and they

shall be one flesh" (Gen. 2:23-24). Then Adam and Eve ate of the tree, i.e., Perfect Knowledge (*Gnosis*). The Saviour appeared to them in the form of an eagle perched in the Tree of Knowledge.

When Yaldabaoth knew they were alienated from him, he cursed. Then, seeing Eve's beauty while she was preparing herself for Adam, he defiled her, begetting Cain and Abel. Then Yaldabaoth implanted the seed of desire in Adam, so that the first parents might bring forth the creatures to be supplied with Yaldabaoth's false spirit. Thus Seth is begotten.

G. The Destinies of Men

John queries the Saviour about Salvation (Doresse thinks the passage is analogous to parts of the *Pistis-Sophia,* and thinks it is an interpolation). "Will all souls be saved, within the pure light?" The Saviour discusses the two "spirits" within man: the Spirit of Life and the false, "Counterfeit," spirit. Those possessing the former go to their reward. Those dominated by the Counterfeit Spirit may also be saved eventually, after a process of reincarnation. Only those who apostatize from Gnosis are un-redeemable. They go to the place reserved for poverty angels, a place of non-repentance, because they have committed the unpardonable sin, blasphemy against the Spirit (Mark 3:29).

The Gnostic explanation of the cosmic scheme goes on with the Demiurge (Yaldabaoth) binding gods, angels, *daimons,* and men to it down to that time. Then Yaldabaoth repents of his creation (cf. Gen. 6:6), and brings the flood on the world. Noah is taught by the Greatness of Light (the Supreme One) to enter into a Light-Cloud (not an ark). Then follows the episode of the angels consorting with the daughters of men, succeeding only when they appear disguised as their husbands and bring them gifts.

The Supreme One (the Metropator) wakens Adam from darkness, descending three times to accomplish this errand. The Saviour instructs John to pass on these secrets to his fellow disciples, but not to sell them for food, drink, raiment, or any such thing. Jesus disappears, and John carries out his commission.

SELECTED BIBLIOGRAPHY

Giversen, Soren. *Apocryphon Johannis* (*Acta Theologica Danica*, V). Copenhagen: Munksgaard, 1963. This is a text edition, with English translation and commentary on the text of Codex II, with *BG.* and Codex III also being consulted.

Grant, Robert M. *Gnosticism: A Source Book of Heretical Writings*
New York: Harper & Bros., 1961.

Helmbold, Andrew K. "The Apocryphon of John," *J.N.E.S.*, XXV
(1966), pp. 258-271. A review of Giversen's work with original
suggestions for improving textual readings and translation.

Jonas, Hans. *Gnostic Religion*. Boston: Beacon Press, 1963
This work, and that of Grant, contains a synopsis of *A.J.* based on
BG. and Irenaeus.

Till, Walter C. "The Gnostic Apocryphon of John," *J.E.H.*, III (1952)
pp. 14-22. This is also based on the shorter version of *BG.* and
Codex III.

VI

THE GOSPEL OF THOMAS

Some scholars think the *Gospel of Thomas* is the most important of the Nag Hammadi texts from the standpoint of New Testament studies. Due to the fact that it was one of the first texts translated and published, it has attained wide fame, being called by some "a fifth gospel," a phrase that is misleading. The work is composed of Logia (Sayings) attributed to Jesus, totaling 112 to 118 according to several variant enumerations. It is not identical with the previously known *Infancy Gospel According to Thomas the Israelite Philosopher*.[1] However, it probably is the same as the *Gospel of Thomas* used by the Manichaeans, and it was known and cited by name by several Church Fathers.[2] The Syriac *Acts of Thomas* may be dependent upon it.

A. THOMAS AND THE OXYRHYNCHUS "LOGIA"

The *Gospel of Thomas* has solved a mystery that has puzzled New Testament scholars many years. What was the nature and source of the sayings of Jesus found in fragmentary papyri at Oxyrhynchus (modern Behnesa), Egypt? The first of these Greek papyri was published in 1897. In 1904 two other fragments, Pap. Oxy. 654 and 655, both by other hands and of a later date, were published. Competent New Testament scholars made many unsuccessful attempts to complete the gaps in the manuscripts.[3] In 1953, Prof. H.-C. Puech identified the *Gospel of Thomas* as the same work as these Oxyrhynchus sayings. To be sure, the Gnostic gospel is written in Coptic, and contains

---

[1]Tr. in M. R. James, *The Apocryphal New Testament*, 1953, pp. 49-57. Cf. Puech, *N. T. Apoc.*, p. 283.

[2]van Unnik, *Newly Discovered Gnostic Writings*, p. 46, cites Origen, *Homily I on Luke* and Cyril of Jerusalem, *Catechesis*, IV.36. Cf. Puech, *N. T. Apoc.*, pp. 283 f.

[3]For a full discussion, cf. Joseph A. Fitzmeyer, "The Oxyrhynchus *Logoi* of Jesus and the Coptic Gospel According to Thomas," *Theological Studies*, XX (1959), pp. 505-560.

Editors at Work on the Text and Translation of the GOSPEL OF THOMAS. Left to right: Henri-Ch. Puech, the late Walter Till, Gilles Quispel, and A. Guillaumont. Missing from the photo is the late Yassah 'abd al-Masih.

some differences in wording as well as some differences in the order of the sayings. The texts, however, are close enough to be certain that they are the same work, perhaps in different recensions or editions. Scholars believe that the Greek version, fragmentarily preserved in the Oxyrhynchus papyri, was less Gnostic than the Coptic version of Nag Hammadi. The correspondences are as follows:

Oxyrhynchus Papyrus No. 1 — seven or eight sayings,[4] Nos. 26-28, 30, 77b, 31-33

Oxyrhynchus Papyrus No. 654 — six sayings, Nos. 1-6

Oxyrhynchus Papyrus No. 655 — four sayings, Nos. 36-39, and two words, probably from Saying No. 24

B. The Nature of Thomas

The *Gospel of Thomas* is unique in literary form. Unlike most apocryphal gospels, it has no narrative framework, but is composed almost entirely of sayings. In that respect it resembles

[4]Here and throughout the enumeration used is that of the *editio princeps* of Guillaumont, *et. al.*

the work which follows it in Codex II, the *Gospel of Philip*. These sayings are loosely connected. In about one-half of the cases the connection is by word association, a phenomenon found also in the synoptic Gospels, as, for example, in Mark 9:34-50. Sayings Nos. 28 and 29 are examples of this type of word association. Here the word *sarx* (flesh) provides the thread. Occasionally sayings are connected by following the order of similar sayings in the canonical Gospels, but sometimes, perversely, *Thomas* inverts the synoptic order. Frequently the subject matter of one saying leads the author to add other sayings dealing with the same theme.

The Passion Week of Christ's life, so strongly emphasized in the canonical Gospels, is entirely omitted in the *Gospel of Thomas*. The stress is not on Jesus as Redeemer, but upon Jesus as Revealer. Deeds and miracles have no part in the *Gospel of Thomas*. It is concerned, not with biography, but with sayings. Most of these either have no introduction by way of narrative, or only a scanty "life situation" is given for them.

While the work as a whole seems to be much nearer orthodox Christianity than most of the Nag Hammadi treatises, with some Sayings seemingly open to an orthodox interpretation, one must proceed with caution in regarding *Thomas* as a sort of half-way house between orthodoxy and heresy. Some sayings are capable of either Christian or Gnostic interpretation. Many are clearly Gnostic. On that basis, as well as on the basis of characteristics enumerated below, it would seem that even those which we can interpret only in an orthodox sense may well have had, to the initiate, a hidden, gnostic meaning. The content of the work is anti-Judaistic, anti-Old Testament, anti-ritualistic, and almost anti-moralistic. The work is not eschatological. In fact one Saying (No. 71) that is futuristic or apocalyptic in the New Testament (Matt. 26:61) is refashioned to take away its futuristic emphasis. Its kingdom of God is not future, but almost exclusively present. As a man "existentially" finds and knows himself, he enters the kingdom.

C. CLASSES OF SAYINGS

The contents of *Thomas* can be catalogued in a number of ways. First of all, they can be classified according to our previous knowledge of the given sayings. Here the content falls into three categories: (1) Those Sayings that are also found in the canonical Gospels. These constitute almost one-half of the book. However, scarcely one of these sayings is completely identical

with the Biblical parallel. Some are quite close; some, far removed. Here one might compare Saying No. 26 with Matthew
7:3-5, Saying No. 34 with Matthew 15:14, and Saying No. 44
with Matthew 12:32. (2) Those sayings that are not in the
Biblical Gospels but known previously from quotations in patristic literature and/or other works in circulation in the early
Christian centuries. A good example here is Saying No. 82,
which was cited by Origen around A.D. 200 (*Exp. Jer.* III, 3).
Saying No. 74 also fits this category (cf. Origen, *Contra Celsum,*
8.15-16). Perhaps as many as twenty sayings belong to this
group. (3) Those sayings that were previously unknown,
nearly forty in all. An example of this type is Saying No. 7:

> Jesus said, "The lion is blessed whom a man shall eat, and the
> lion shall become a man, and the man is cursed whom the lion
> shall eat, and the lion shall become a man" (following Coptic
> text).

The possibility that genuine *agrapha* (previously unknown sayings) of Jesus may be found in *Thomas* cannot be rejected
since the canonical Gospels (cf. Luke 1:1; John 20:30) specifically say they are not exhaustive.[5]

Classified according to type or form, the Sayings of the
Gospel of Thomas can be grouped as follows: (1) Parables.
Some scholars have seen as many as twenty-four parables in
Thomas, but Gartner lists only fourteen: Sayings Nos. 8, 9, 20,
21a, 57, 63, 64, 65, 76, 96, 97, 98, 107, 109.[6] Most of these are
known already in the synoptic Gospels. Naturally these have
been the object of much study. (2) Beatitudes. The following
Sayings are parallels to New Testament passages: Sayings Nos.
54, 68, 69a, 69b. However, some of *Thomas'* beatitudes are un-
known to the New Testament: Sayings Nos. 19, 49, 58, 103. (3)
Woes. These are not the same as those of the New Testament,
but may be patterned after them. Two such woes occur: Sayings
Nos. 102 and 112. (4) Programmatic Sayings ("I shall . . . I
come to . . ."). These sayings, like those of the Gospels, give
us the "program" of Jesus, His purpose in His ministry. Sayings
Nos. 71, 10 and 23 are programmatic sayings. (5) Dialogue.
Speakers named in the *Gospel of Thomas* are Peter, Matthew,
Thomas, Mariham (Mary), Salome, and simply "the disciples."
Most frequently the dialogues in *Thomas* take the form of

---

[5]Bertil Gartner, *The Theology of the Gospel According to Thomas,* pp. 49 ff.
[6]*Ibid.,* p. 18.

questions and answers. These interrogations and their responses are typically Gnostic in content. Since an original expository work, *The Epistle of Eugnostos,* gives evidence of being reworked into a dialogue framework and presented as a separate work, namely, the *Wisdom of Jesus Christ* (both works are in the Nag Hammadi find), some think the same may be true of *Thomas.* This would infer that the author took canonical sayings to which he could give a Gnostic "twist" and added to them extra-canonical sayings and apocryphal sayings that were already definitely Gnostic. At any rate, the *Wisdom of Jesus Christ* and the *Apocryphon of John,* both second-century documents from Nag Hammadi, as well as the third-century *Pistis Sophia,* demonstrate the Gnostic fondness for the dialogue style. However, it should be observed that the literary forms used in *Thomas* are common in non-gnostic apocryphal gospels.

Another system of classification — albeit an incomplete one — calls attention to the mechanical structure of the various sayings. Some of the sayings are doublets. Examples of this are: the world as a corpse, Sayings Nos. 56 and 80; body and soul, Sayings Nos. 87 and 112; the Kingdom of God is within, Sayings Nos. 2 and 113; "I came to cast a fire," Sayings Nos. 10 and 16; hating one's family, Sayings Nos. 55 and 101; parable of the robbers, Sayings Nos. 21b and 103; power to move mountains, Sayings Nos. 48 and 106.

Some of the Sayings are shorter in Coptic than they are in the Greek (Oxyrhynchus papyri) version, and/or in the Greek New Testament. An instance here is Saying No. 36. Saying No. 5 is the same as in the New Testament, but both vary from the Oxyrhynchus text. It is also noteworthy that some Sayings are conflated texts. The author took a text from the synoptic Gospels and added to it. An example of this is Saying No. 44 compared with Matthew 12:32. Still other Sayings are compound texts. The author combined parallel Sayings or related Sayings from two Gospels into one Saying. An example is Saying No. 24. This reworking of Biblical material is satirized by Irenaeus. He says (*Adv. Haer.* I.8.1) the Gnostics are like a man who took a mosaic portrait of a king, broke it apart and rearranged the pieces to make a picture of a dog or a fox, then called the new composition the king's portrait. Since Marcion reduced the number of Gospels in his canon to one (Luke), and Tatian attempted to harmonize the four Gospels in his *Diatesseron* (*ca.* A.D. 170), the *Gospel of Thomas* may be another example of this tendency.

D. AUTHORSHIP AND DATE

In the Gospel of John we read of Thomas who is called Didymus (John 11:16; 20:24; 21:2). Here John is translating the Aramaic "Thomas" into Greek, "Didymus," both meaning "twin." The *Gospel of Thomas* (in Coptic, not in the Greek Oxyrhynchus version) is ignorant of this translation, so gives its author's full name as Didymus Judas Thomas. Evidently the apostle Thomas held a high place in Gnostic thought. In fact, the Gnostics believed that special revelations had been given to Matthias, Thomas, and Philip, who thus stand vis-à-vis the canonical inner circle of Peter, James, and John. In this same codex that contains the *Gospel of Thomas* is found the *Book of Thomas the Athlete*, which, reputedly, is a work by Matthias. The apocryphal *Acts of Thomas*, dated in the first quarter of the third century A.D., which Puech thinks is based on the *Gospel of Thomas*, describes Thomas' missionary activity in the East. This same work clearly depicts Thomas as the twin brother of Jesus.[7] This connection of Thomas with the East is also referred to in the *Book of Thomas the Athlete*. One old Syrian manuscript reads "Judas Thomas" at John 14:22 instead of merely "Judas." All this evidence for the prominence of Thomas in the Syrian church would point to that area, possibly the city of Edessa, as the source for the original writing of *Thomas*. Some feel it was originally written in Syriac, and that both the Greek and Coptic versions are translations. Again, the agreements between the Syriac versions of the New Testament, the *Diatesseron* of Tatian, and the *Gospel of Thomas* point to the Syriac origin. These agreements will be evaluated later.

The Gospel of Thomas cannot be dated with as much accuracy as one would wish. It must have been in existence before A.D. 225, which is the latest date possible for the Oxyrhynchus papyri. The *Gospel of the Hebrews*, evidently one of the sources for *Thomas*, was in existence before A.D. 150. Some of the best information now available leads one to date *Thomas* somewhere between A.D. 140 and 170.

E. GNOSTIC SOURCES

The contents of the *Gospel of Thomas* are closely related to Gnostic ideas in a number of sects: Ophites, Naasenes, Valen-

---

[7] van Unnik, *op. cit.*, p. 49, quotes *Acts of Thomas*, ch. 39, "Twin brother of the Messiah, apostle of the Most-High, and fellow initiate in the hidden words of the Messiah, who hast received his secret pronouncements." Peuch, *N.T. Apoc.*, p. 287.

inians, even Basilidians. Gartner prefers to think *Thomas* came from a Valentinian source.[8] However, the weight of evidence from quotations of *Thomas* in patristic literature attributing it to the Naasenes favors the conclusion that it was composed and first used by that group. One must remember, furthermore, that these Gnostic groups were not as far apart as one might be led to believe. The most extreme Gnostic groups were not nearly so far removed from each other as, for example, a Greek Orthodox churchman is from a Pentecostalist — both classified as Christian! Hippolytus (*ca.* A.D. 235) in *Refutations* V.7.20 says that the Naasenes used the *Gospel of Thomas,* citing a curious variant of Saying No. 4. In *Refutations* V.8.32 he attributes to the Naasenes a saying that is almost identical to *Thomas,* Saying No. 11. Again, we know that *Thomas* used the *Gospel of the Hebrews,* and that this gospel was popular in Naasene circles. The interweaving of Biblical texts is also typically Naasene, but not exclusively so.

Mention has just been made of the *Gospel of the Hebrews,* which is no longer extant. Clement of Alexandria, about A.D. 200, in *Stromata* II.9.45 cited Saying No. 2 in a variant form as coming from *Hebrews.*[9] There is also a possibility that Sayings Nos. 12, 14, and 104 may be related to this lost apocryphal gospel. At any rate, the *Gospel of Thomas* may help recover something more of this lost work. Another apocryphal gospel, more definitely Gnostic, also reappears in the Nag Hammadi book of *Thomas.* This is the *Gospel of the Egyptians,* but is not identical with the book of that name in the Nag Hammadi corpus. Rather it is the work mentioned in Clement's *Stromata* III.13.92 and III.63.2, passages that have definite relationships to Sayings Nos. 22, 37, and 61.

F. Thomas and the Fathers

Other Church Fathers show knowledge of *Thomas.* Irenaeus (*Epideixis* 43) cites Saying No. 19. Origen rejected the *Gospel of Thomas* in his *Homily on Jeremiah* 3.3, a passage referring to Saying No. 82. Augustine in *Com. adversus legis et prophetas* 2.14, referring to Saying No. 52, also rejects *Thomas.*[10]

---

[8]*Op. cit.,* p. 272. Cf. Grant-Freedman, pp. 78 f., who cite Saying No. 38 as Valentinian.

[9]Cf. van Unnik, *op. cit.,* p. 51, and Grant-Freedman, p. 71.

[10]Cf. Grant-Freedman, pp. 28-59, and *passim* the commentary for a convenient discussion of *Thomas* and its relation to other apocryphal literature.

G. RELATION TO CANONICAL GOSPELS

Christian readers of the *Gospel of Thomas* are interested — rightly or wrongly — not so much in what religious ideas it presented, but how it relates to the canonical Gospels. This relationship, in those passages that show one, takes several forms. The introductory formula used by Thomas, "Jesus said," is evidently borrowed from the frequent use of "He said to them," or similar expressions in Mark 4:13, 21, 24, 26, 30, and elsewhere. The Gospels most commonly used by *Thomas* are the three synoptics, with only a scanty reference to John. He dwells on Matthew 5-7, 13, and Luke 6, 11, and 12. Among the synoptics, *Thomas* prefers Luke, and uses practically nothing that is peculiar to Mark alone. However, no straight line relationship can be set forth, for while he usually follows Luke, sometimes he prefers Matthew. For example, in Saying No. 26 *Thomas* prefers to follow Matthew 3:3 ff., rather than the longer version in Luke 6:41 ff. Saying No. 34 is based on Matthew 15:14. Saying No. 44 is an elaboration of Matthew 12:32 (incidentally, the theme here is a Gnostic favorite, cf. *A.J.*). Some Sayings are completely different from the canonical parallels, cf. Sayings Nos. 15 and 87. The discovery of *Thomas* has brought out the question of its relationship to the hypothetical common source, aside from Mark, of Matthew and Luke, a source called "Q" by the scholars. This source, however, had narrative framework, which, as we have seen, is lacking in *Thomas*.

Another problem posed by *Thomas* is that concerning variant readings in the Greek New Testament as they relate to Sayings in *Thomas*. It seems quite evident that *Thomas* fits into the scheme of the so-called Western text of the New Testament. This text family includes the old Syriac versions, the *Diatesseron*, Codex Beza, Old Latin, and other manuscripts. Quispel found one hundred parallels between *Thomas* and the *Diatesseron* which Tatian completed *ca.* A.D. 170.[11] For example, Saying No. 54 may reflect the text used by Tatian. It would seem that *Thomas* and its congeries in the Western family followed one textual tradition, while the Greek manuscripts that are the basis of the textus receptus and most more recent Greek New Testaments followed another textual tradition.[12] Again, there are

[11]Gilles Quispel, "L'Evangile selon Thomas et le Diatesseron," *V.C.,* XIII (1959), pp. 87 ff.
[12]Gilles Quispel, "Some Remarks on the Gospel of Thomas," *New Testament Studies,* V (1959), p. 282.

many parallels to the *Pseudo-Clementines,* which were in circulation among Jewish Christians. These *Pseudo-Clementines,* in turn, were known to Justin who was a teacher of Tatian. So the thought world in which *Thomas* was produced was evidently a Syriac- or Aramaic-speaking, semi-Christian community outside Palestine about mid-second century.

SELECTED BIBLIOGRAPHY

Gärtner, Bertil. *The Theology of the Gospel of Thomas.* New York: Harper and Bro., 1961.

Grant, Robert M. and Freedman, David Noel. *The Secret Sayings of Jesus According to the Gospel of Thomas.* Garden City: Doubleday, 1961.

Guillaumont, Antoine, *et. al. The Gospel According to Thomas.* New York: Harper and Bro., 1959.

Turner, H. E. W. and Montefiore, Hugh W. *Thomas and the Evangelists.* Naperville: Allenson, 1962.

Wilson, Robert McL. *Studies in the Gospel of Thomas.* London: Mowbray, 1960.

VII

THE GOSPEL OF PHILIP

Many mysteries surround this Gnostic "Gospel." Among the questions it poses are the following: precisely who is being addressed by its author? Is the Apostle Philip the author? Exactly when was it written? Exactly what does it say in some crucial passages? What does it mean in some passages that are clearly worded? Nevertheless, what can be stated with certainty about this gospel far exceeds what must, at this date, remain obscure. It seems evident that the Coptic work is not identical with the *Gospel of Philip* cited by Epiphanius (*Panarion,* xxvi. 13. 2-3).[1] What then can we say affirmatively about it?

A. NATURE AND BACKGROUND

The thirty-six pages of text of *Philip* constitute a continuous discourse, or exposition, consisting of 127 Sayings or sermonettes.[2] It is not clear whether *Philip* is a collection (as *Thomas* seems to be), or an original composition by someone posing as the disciple Philip, or partly a collection and partly an original composition. Gartner calls *Philip* "a compendium of doctrinal passages drawn from Gnostic sources."[3] However, one must keep in mind that the doctrinal passages were being used homiletically, and that the author of *Philip* may have been the originator of much of the Gnostic gospel. Many of the Sayings are amplifications or explanations of Scriptural passages along Gnostic lines.

---

[1]However, Doresse, *Secret Books,* p. 225, says the passage given by the heresiologist is found in another Nag Hammadi text, *The Gospel of the Egyptians!* Puech, *N.T. Apoc.,* I, p. 273, says it was cited by Epiphanius, but cf. p. 277.

[2]Following the enumeration of Schenke in Leipoldt-Schenke, *Koptisch-gnostische Schriften aus den Papyrus-Codices von Nag Hammadi,* also followed by Wilson, *The Gospel of Philip.*

[3]Bertil Gartner, *The Theology of the Gospel According to Thomas,* p. 30.

The GOSPEL OF THOMAS and the GOSPEL OF PHILIP. This photo shows the closing page of the GOSPEL OF THOMAS, including the colophon PEUAGGELION PKATA THOMAS, and the opening lines of the GOSPEL OF PHILIP.

The Sayings of *Philip* vary from two to fifty-eight lines of text, therefore they are usually longer than those in *Thomas*. The longest Saying (No. 123) goes to fifty-eight lines, while in *Thomas* the longest Saying (No. 64) takes only twenty-six lines. Rather than compare *Philip* with *Thomas*, perhaps one should compare it with the *Gospel of Truth* since both seem to fit a loose classification of homilies. *Philip* resembles Proverbs 1-9 in its cohesiveness, while *Thomas* is similar to Proverbs 10-31. As in *Thomas*, so in *Philip*, Sayings are strung together by word association (Nos. 4 and 5, "dying, dead"; Nos. 23 and 24, "clothing, garments"), and by association of ideas (Nos. 10 and 11, deceptiveness of names; Nos. 112 and 113, like begets like).

While Doresse[4] thinks *Philip* came from Judeo-Christian circles, it seems clear that the Judeo-Christian background is remote. The immediate background seems to be within Valen-

[4]*Op. cit.*, p. 225.

tinianism.[5] In Valentinian doctrine the Lower Sophia, the last emanation of the Pleroma, is called Achamoth. Philip calls the higher Sophia "Echamoth," and the lower Sophia "Echmoth" (Saying No. 39). (Actually, the Greek *sophia* is the same as the Hebrew *hochmoth*, both meaning "wisdom," so there is no reason why both higher and lower Sophia should not have the same name.) Furthermore, it is in Valentinianism that there is stress on the "mystery" of marriage, i.e., the reunion of souls within the Pleroma, a theme constantly recurring in *Philip*. While accepting the Valentinian origins of *Philip*, one must not be blind to its many parallels to other schools of Gnosticism. For example, relationship to the Barbelo-gnostics is shown by the parallels between Sayings in *Philip* and passages in the *Apocryphon of John*. For its interpretation, *Philip* — in contradistinction to *Thomas*[6] — needs no other keys than a knowledge of the New Testament and the teachings of the Valentinians.

It seems likely that the original of *Philip* was written in Greek. Yet it is evident that the writer was well acquainted with a Semitic milieu, for there seem to be some glosses that comment on the Syriac or Hebrew meanings of certain names. The entire text in Codex II occupies thirty-five pages. It is quite well preserved except for the bottoms of the pages. Pages 112-122 each have up to 15 lines extensively damaged, while the remaining twenty-four pages have six to eight lines of text in a fragmentary state. This makes reconstructions of these lines difficult in most cases, and in some instances practically impossible. The conjectures of Schenke are the result of much labor but, for the most part, remain conjectures.[7]

B. AUTHORSHIP AND DATE

A third-century Gnostic work, *Pistis Sophia* (ch. 42), says that Philip, Thomas, and Matthias were disciples to whom Jesus had committed the responsibility of putting His secret revelations into writing.[8] This tripartite division of labor is based on Deuteronomy 19:15. In the *Wisdom of Jesus Christ* only Philip, Thomas, and Matthew, plus Bartholomew and Mariamme are

---

[5]Cf. Schenke in Leipoldt-Schenke, pp. 34 ff. and Wilson, *op. cit.*, pp. 6, 20.

[6]One need only examine the expositions of *Thomas* by Grant-Freedman and Gartner to see the difficulties in the interpretation of that work.

[7]These are discussed by Martin Krause in his review of Walter Till's *Das Evangelium nach Philippos* in *Z.K.G.*, I/II (1964), pp. 168-184. Schenke restates and modifies his suggestions in an article in *TLZ*, XC (1965), col. 321-332.

[8]The passage is cited in full by Doresse, *op. cit.*, pp. 221 f. and Puech, *N.T. Apoc.*, I, p. 272.

engaged in conversation with the Saviour. Perhaps, as Doresse surmises,[9] Philip's name is attached to this Gnostic work because the Biblical Philip baptized Simon of Samaria (Acts 8: 12 f.), who was regarded by some as the founder of Gnosticism. Others think that Philip's name was given to this work because he is the only disciple mentioned in it. Since it seems evident that the Gnostics wished to get their writings accepted by attributing their authorship to Biblical personalities, it appears likely that this consideration was at work with *Philip*. At any rate, the writer considers himself to be a Christian (Sayings Nos. 6, 102; cf. also Nos. 49, 59, 67), and to be in the Apostolic tradition (Saying No. 47). This feature helps to date the book. It would be increasingly difficult to make this claim after the time of Irenaeus (*ca.* A.D. 180).

As yet there seems to be no consensus of opinion as to the date of the original composition of *Philip*. Puech dates it from the second or early third century.[10] This is because it agrees with what was known in that period about Valentinianism as attested by Irenaeus (*Adv. Haer.*) and Clement of Alexandria (*Excerpta ex Theodota*). Wilson seems to oscillate between a mid-second-century date, prior to *Thomas, ca.* A.D. 150, and a late second-century date, 175-200, when Valentinianism was quite far advanced.[11] In any event, the work seems well removed from late first-century Judeo-Christianity, and prior to the fantastic Gnostic speculations of the third and fourth centuries.

C. LITERARY TYPES

As in *Thomas,* so in *Philip,* one can discern three types of Sayings. Some are almost exact quotations of the New Testament. Other Sayings are related to the New Testament but more or less removed — some being merely faint echoes. The third type embraces Sayings unrelated to the New Testament, but they are recognized as similar to or identical with passages quoted in the Church Fathers or found in other Gnostic works. Being a homily, *Philip* lacks the dialogue style so frequent in *Thomas.* Its author, as a good preacher, makes extensive use of figures of speech to illustrate his points. He refers to the good dyer, the glass blower, the structure of the Jerusalem temple, and the ass turning the mill. (As Wilson, citing Segelberg, points out, this would make a good sermon topic entitled "Don-

---

[9]*Secret Books,* p. 222 note.
[10]*N.T. Apoc.,* I, p. 278.
[11]*Gospel of Philip,* p. 11, but *contra* this cf. p. 23.

key Religion.") One of his favorite devices is the use of comparison, frequently in the explicit formula "as . . . so." Another typical device of *Philip* is the use of contrasts. This is especially pronounced in Sayings Nos. 1-7 where one encounters the following pairs: slave and son, dead and living, Gentile and Gnostic, Hebrew and Christian, summer and winter, sowing and reaping.

D. BIBLICAL RELATIONSHIPS

The writer of *Philip* drew extensively on the Gospels of Matthew and John. This use of John reminds one of the Evangelist's popularity with the author of the *Gospel of Truth*. Of Paul's writings, the author of *Philip* certainly used Romans, I and II Corinthians, Galatians, and Philippians. Some passages are allusions to or citations of Hebrews, I Peter, and I John. As with the *Gospel of Truth* and *Thomas*, the total impression one gets is that the author of *Philip* was a man immersed in Scripture. To make use of the New Testament so naturally requires intimate acquaintance. Such acquaintance, in turn, shows how the "great Gnostics" must have arisen from Christian or Judeo-Christian circles, and how the line of demarcation between orthodoxy and heresy was non-existent or exceedingly fine in the second century prior to Irenaeus.

The content of *Philip* aids the Biblical scholar at three points to be discussed in the final chapter: (1) The *Gospel of Philip* reveals that when Philip wrote, the canon was practically identical with that later "officially" laid down. (2) *Philip* shows something of the history of exegesis.[12] (3) *Philip* provides several instances of textual variants from the *textus receptus,* both agreeing with manuscripts of the Western family of texts.

E. THEMES

The predominant themes on which the writer of *Philip* "rings the changes" are (1) Adam and Paradise, (2) creation versus begetting, (3) redemption, (4) the Gnostic Sacraments, and (5) the "mystery" of the bridal chamber. Although most of these themes are doctrines found in the early church, *Philip's* exposition of them is not in accordance with the Bible, nor does it agree with Christian theology of the latter half of the second century. For example, Adam's death is not due to sin (Rom. 6:23), but to the separation of the male principle from the

---

[12]*Ibid.,* p. 190.

female (Sayings Nos. 71 and 78; cf. *A.J.*, Codex II, 69.12-14).
Because this world is unreal (Sayings Nos. 10, 11, 63), and was
created through transgression (as in *A.J.*), man must escape to
the other Aeon. As the Bible, *Philip* teaches the negation of the
flesh (Sayings Nos. 22, 62, 123), but for a far different motive.
Likewise, sacrifice (Sayings Nos. 14 and 50) and idolatry (Sayings Nos. 84 and 85) are condemned, again from a different
motivation. As in the *Apocryphon of John*, God is a transcendent
Being, utterly unknowable to man. Man is created and placed in
Paradise, then falls into sin. He is redeemed, not by the cross,
but by knowledge (*gnosis*) (Sayings Nos. 110 and 115), especially the knowledge of the "mysteries" (sacraments). These
"mysteries" reach their culmination in the Sacrament of the
Bridal Chamber where, symbolically at least, the separation is
remedied. While Christ is referred to at least twenty-seven
times, and six other passages seem to refer to Him by the title
of "Son" or "Son of Man," *Philip* contains no theory of the atone-
ment, and places no saving merit in the cross. Christ came,
rather, to restore things to their place (Saying No. 70), and "to
remove the separation" (Saying No. 78). Man receives deliverance from bondage (Saying No. 110), but that bondage is
ignorance and forgetfulness (as in *A.J.*), not captivity to an alien
power residing in him (cf. Rom. 7). Man needs faith, hope,
and love (I Cor. 13), but more important is knowledge (*gnosis*)
(Saying No. 115). Truly, *Philip* knows the New Testament
language, but is far from understanding its meaning.

F. SACRAMENTS

According to *Philip* there were five sacraments. Saying No. 68
enumerates Baptism, Chrism (anointing), Eucharist (Lord's
Supper), Redemption, and the Bridal Chamber. Apparently,
more stress was placed on the first two and the last. Baptism
was by immersion (Sayings Nos. 59, 101, 109, and possibly 89).
The Holy Spirit was supposedly received at Baptism (Saying
No. 59), not at Confirmation as in the Eastern church generally.
Baptism gave the initiate an unchangeable character (Saying
No. 43).

The Chrism was superior to Baptism according to Saying No.
95 (also Saying No. 76 according to one restoration). Here one
may note that the Marcosians regarded Baptism as merely
"psychic" (the perfect Gnostic was a cut higher, "pneumatic");
cf. Irenaeus (*Adv. Haer.* i.21.2) and Hippolytus (*Ref.* vi. 41.2-4,
42.1). Perhaps what the heresiologists call *apolutrosis* (Redemp-

tion) was the equivalent of Chrism, or possibly the two sacraments were fused into one rite (a modern parallel would be Confirmation and First Communion). Olive oil was used in the Chrism according to Saying No. 92.

The Eucharist is mentioned in Sayings Nos. 15, 23 (both passages contain phrases reminiscent of John 6), 53, 98, 100, and 108. The latter three have phrases reminiscent of I Corinthians 10. In Saying No. 98 there may be some connection between the Eucharist and the Redemption, a connection that seems to fit in with the picture of the Valentinian Marcosian rite described by Irenaeus (*Adv. Haer.* i.21.4). The rite of Redemption is also associated with the Marcosians in *Adv. Haer.* i.29. Redemption may have some connection with Baptism in Saying No. 76. Unfortunately, the lacuna in the text at this point precludes certainty.

There is ample Biblical background for the final Sacrament — the Bridal Chamber. In the Old Testament the relationship of God and Israel was likened to bride and groom (cf. Hosea's experience), and in the New Testament (Eph. 5:21-32) Christ and the church have a similar relationship. However, in Gnostic thought this relationship was transposed into another realm. Archetypically, Christ was the Bridegroom, the Sophia was the Bride, and the Pleroma was the Bridal Chamber. The redeemed man was reunited with his angel consort within the Pleroma. Evidently, the Valentinians made much of this idea. In fact, Clement of Alexandria (*Stromata,* iii. 4.29) said they talked of "acts of spiritual union." Just what took place in the Sacrament itself is not clear. It would seem reasonable to infer that there was some sort of re-enactment of the archetypical situation. In the light of such a possible re-enactment, and the fact that Sayings Nos. 76 and 77 refer to sacraments (and Saying No. 78 only sets the stage for Saying No. 79), perhaps Saying No. 79, "The woman is united to her husband in the bridal chamber," is to be understood as the sacrament taken quite literally. Events within the bridal chamber would be "symbolic action." When *Philip* speaks of marriage it is difficult to tell whether one is to interpret him literally, or to interpret the Saying as referring to this Sacrament.

SELECTED BIBLIOGRAPHY

De Catanzaro, C. J. "The Gospel According to Philip," *J.T.S.,* XII (1962), pp. 35-71. (Contains an English translation of the Coptic text.)

Grant, Robert M. "Two Gnostic Gospels," *J.B.L.*, LXXIX (1960), pp. 1-11.

—————————. "The Mystery of Marriage in the Gospel of Philip," *V.C.*, XV (1961), pp. 129 ff.

Helmbold, Andrew K. "Translation Problems in the Gospel of Philip," *New Testament Studies*, X (1964), pp. 93-97.

van Unnik, W. C. "Three Notes on the Gospel of Philip," *New Testament Studies*, X (1964), pp. 465-469.

Wilson, Robert McL. *The Gospel of Philip*. New York: Harper and Row, 1962.

VIII

THE REMAINDER OF CODEX II

Four works from Codex II remain to be discussed: *The Hypostasis of the Archons*, a Sethian treatise without title, *The Exegesis of the Soul*, and *The Book of Thomas the Athlete*. The Coptic text with German translation of the Sethian treatise has been published.[1] In addition, German translations of the *Hypostasis* and the Sethian treatise have appeared.[2] Editions and full translations of the other two works are promised.[3] Therefore the discussion of these texts, except the *Hypostasis*, will be limited to relating what others have said concerning them. The text of *The Hypostasis of the Archons* is readily accessible through the photocopies in *Coptic Gnostic Papyri*, Vol. I, so its contents can be dealt with in more detail.

A. The Hypostasis (Essence) of the Archons

Like the *Gospel of Thomas* and the *Gospel of Truth*, this work derives its English title from its opening words "Concerning the Hypostasis of the Powers in the Spirit of the Father of Truth." However, the following untitled work twice mentions "the preceding book of Norea," so perhaps the original readers of the *Hypostasis* called it *The Book of Norea*. Norea, in this work, is

---

[1] Alexander Bohlig and Pahor Labib, *Die koptisch-gnostische Schrift ohne Titel aus Codex II von Nag Hammadi (Veroffentlichungen d. Inst. f. Orientf. d. Deutschen Akademie d. Wiss.* Nr. 58) (Berlin, 1962).

[2] Hans Martin Schenke, "Das Wesen der Archonten. Eine gnostische Originalschrift aus dem Funde von Nag Hammadi," *TLZ*, LXXXIII (1958), col. 661-670, also reproduced in J. Leipoldt-H. M. Schenke, *Koptisch-gnostische Schriften*, pp. 69-78. H. M. Schenke, "Vom Ursprung der Welt. Eine titellose gnostische Abhandlung aus dem Funde von Nag Hammadi, *TLZ*, LXXXIV (1959), col. 243-256.

[3] J. Martin Plumley, *The Hypostasis of the Archons*. Martin Krause and Pahor Labib, *Gnostische und hermetische Schriften aus Codex II und VI*. Roger A. Bullard's dissertation, *The Hypostasis of the Archons: The Coptic Text with Translation and Commentary*, is tentatively scheduled for publication in the *Patristische Texte und Studien* series (Berlin: de Gruyter, 1967).

the wife of Noah. Doresse thinks that our current work may really be an abridgment of the original *Book of Norea*,[4] which is mentioned by Irenaeus (*Adv. Haer.* I.30). The work itself seems to be a little later than the other compositions in the Codex, coming, probably, from the third century A.D. Nothing is known concerning its authorship, except that the content indicates it came from a Sethian circle.

The myth described in the *Hypostasis* is very close to what Irenaeus describes of the Ophites/Sethians in *Adv. Haer.* I, 30. Doresse points out that the myth is similar to what is found in the long-since discovered Gnostic text, *Pistis Sophia*.[5] The central events of the supposed *Book of Norea* are summarized in Epiphanius (*Ref.* xxvi.). A study of the *Hypostasis* reveals that it is close to the *Apocryphon of John* in its mythology, or perhaps one should say demonology or Pleromatology, but the *Hypostasis* differs in some important points.

The work opens with a citation of Ephesians 6:12. This introduces the "powers" (*edzousia*) who are the Gnostic Archons. As in the *Apocryphon of John*, Yaldabaoth plays a central role. In fact, the passage in which Yaldabaoth displays his conceit and ignorance by saying, "I am God. There is no one except me" is almost word for word parallel to the *Apocryphon*. The reply given to him is, "You have erred, Samael." The text explains that this name, Samael, means "the God of the Blind."

Upon seeing the likeness of Indestructibility in the water (i.e., the image of God), the Archons decide to make a man of the dust of the earth in the image of God. They say, as in Genesis, "Let us make man. . . ." Doing so, they produce a man who is merely psychic. This man, Adam, then names all the beasts for the Archons. He is placed in Paradise to till it and guard it. He is forbidden to eat from the tree of knowledge (*gnosis*) whereby he could escape their clutches.

The Archons put Adam to sleep, as in Genesis. They extract Eve (also called Zoe or Life) from him, and she gives Adam life — pneumatic or spiritual life. The Archons then try to defile her. Here the story differs from the *Apocryphon of John* in that she substitutes her shadow with whom they disport. As in Genesis, the serpent tempts Eve by denying the truth of God's warning, "dying ye shall die." She yields to the temptation, and gives the fruit to Adam also. They recognize their condition and make fig leaf aprons. The Archons cast them out of

---

[4]Jean Doresse, *Secret Books*, p. 163.
[5]*Ibid.*, p. 159.

The Untitled Work of Codex II. This photo of page 111 shows the position of the pages in the bindings.

Paradise. They beget Cain and Abel (again at variance with *A.J.*). Cain murders his brother Abel, and Seth and Norea are born. The name Norea may be connected with the Semitic root *nur*, "to shine." She plays somewhat the same role as Pyrrha, the wife of Deucalion in Greek mythology. It is not yet clear what relation she may have to Nuraitha, who is the wife of Noah in the Mandaean *Johannesbuch* and *Ginza*.

Next follows the flood episode. The Archons advise Noah to make an ark, a literal craft (not as in *A.J.*, a "demythologized" ark) which is to be put on Mount Seir. This may have some connection with the Mount Nisir of *Gilgamesh Epic,* xi.144 (the Babylonian flood story).[6] Old Noah disbars Norea from the ark because she is of the perfect generation, a motif that may be related to the "sons of God, daughters of men" ideology of Genesis 6:2. In anger she burns the ark. The Archons try to defile her, but are repulsed. She seeks and receives assistance from the great angel, Eleleth. He is one of the four great lights

---

[6]For English translation see Alexander Heidel, *The Gilgamesh Epic and Old Testament Parallels* (Chicago: University of Chicago Press, 1949). Cf. Doresse, *op. cit.,* p. 161 n., for a discussion of the Gnostic passage.

(wisdom) as in the *Apocryphon of John,* but there he is over the souls of those ignorant of the Pleroma. In response to her questions, Eleleth tells her from what Hypostasis the Archons (*edzousia*) originated.

The treatise then reverts to pre-history. It tells of Sophia's wish to beget without the consent of her consort. She produces an aborted form from the darkness beneath the veil below the Pleroma.[7] This abortion is a self-willed, lion-beast, male-female, who boasts "I am God." Thus Yaldabaoth comes on the scene. This self-willed one (as in *A.J.*) then creates his seven Aeons or Sons (described as male-female, but not so specified in *A.J.*). Yaldabaoth is bound by an angel from the breath of Zoe. He is cast into Tartarus. His son, Sabaoth, repents, praising Pistis and Zoe. Sabaoth, thereupon, is set in the seventh heaven, beneath the veil. Sabaoth is given a four-faced cherubim chariot (derived from Ezekiel?) with a multitude of angels surrounding it. This motif is also found in the following Sethian treatise and in Codex Bruce. It may be connected with Jewish speculation concerning the Divine Throne (*Merkeba*).[8]

The work closes with Sophia causing Zoe to be seated at the right of Sabaoth and an angel (Eleleth?) to be seated on his left. Yaldabaoth is jealous of his son's glory. The redeemed sons of Light cry out, as in Revelation, "Holy, Holy, Holy."

B. The Untitled Sethian Treatise

This work seems to be related to at least two other texts found at Nag Hammadi. We have already noted that it refers to the *Book of Norea* as the source of some of its ideas, and Doresse is of the opinion that the *Hypostasis of the Archons* is an abridgment of that *Book.* He also claims that the more didactic or formalized doctrinal exposition of the untitled work was derived from the *Epistle of Eugnostos,* found in Codex V.[9] It should be noted that kinship of ideas — even the presence of long, identical passages — is no guarantee of a genealogical relationship. Both may come from a common source, or simply reflect a common oral tradition.

Doresse thinks the text is very much interpolated, so that it now contains many commentaries and glosses on the original.[10] Oftentimes these interpolations are of the nature of bibliographi-

---

[7]Doresse, *op. cit.,* p. 162.
[8]*Ibid.,* pp. 290 ff.
[9]*Ibid.,* p. 195.
[10]*Ibid.,* p. 170.

cal references. Some passages seem to imply knowledge of, and/ or documentation in the *Testament of Solomon, Archangelike of Moses the Prophet,* and the *Book of Norea.* Some other bibliographical references are as yet unidentified with previously known works, but may refer to Nag Hammadi Gnostic texts that have not yet been edited and studied.

The work is basically a theogony and cosmology setting forth Pistis Sophia as its central character. The world began with the Immortals. One of these, Pistis, also called Sophia, developed a work between the Immortals and the things below (i.e., outside the Pleroma). From Darkness and obscurity, Chaos came forth. Darkness became jealous, and the Abyss filled with waters. Seeing that these waters did not have the essential element — the Spirit — Pistis was terrified. This fear produced upon the waters the monstrous figure Yaldabaoth, who was also called Ariel, i.e., "the lion of God." It is instructive to note that Sophia's emotion which produced the Demiurge was fear, not passion as in the *Apocryphon of John* and other Gnostic texts. In this work, as in the *Apocryphon,* Yaldabaoth thought he alone existed, and he created powers to be beneath him. Unlike the *Apocryphon,* they were not limited to twelve, nor were they given the same names. One of his seven sons was Sabaoth. The other powers he created included thrones, powers, and archangels. When Yaldabaoth made his insolent boast about there being no god before him, a light came from the Ogdoad and appeared before him in the form of a Man (the Primeval Man?). In the *Apocryphon* this is paralleled by the voice that responds to Yaldabaoth's boast by saying, "Man exists, and the Son of Man." Yaldabaoth's consort, the Pronoia, fell in love with this Man who spurned her.

Sabaoth, as in the *Hypostasis,* turned against his father, and exalted Pistis Sophia. As a reward Sabaoth received a place of rest in the seventh heaven. Yaldabaoth became jealous of his son's exalted position. At this point the published text ends.

One further point of interest in this Sethian work can be mentioned. At 151.24 Pistis tells Yaldabaoth, "Thou with thine shall descend to thy Mother, the Deep." This reading confirms the theory that the name of the Demiurge means "child of Chaos."

C. THE EXEGESIS OF THE SOUL

This work is not a prophetic revelation, but rather a long treatise by some anonymous writer. Its opening scenes are

eminiscent of ideas set forth in Zosimos' *On the Letter Omega.*
Doresse thinks it is full of "eclectic glosses and references."[11]
The writer quotes from Hosea and Psalms, as well as from
pagan classics. He cites Homer's *Odyssey* (as do the Naasenes
according to the *Philosopheumena,* and as Simon Magus used
he myth of Circe according to the same source). Eustathius'
commentary on the *Odyssey* discloses why this poem fascinated
the Gnostics. Calypso is an allegory of the body enclosing the
soul like a shell. Reason (i.e., Hermes) enables Ulysses to break
the thralldom and return to the intelligible world. This is all
clearly allied to Gnostic thought.

D. THE BOOK OF THOMAS THE ATHLETE

The title of the closing treatise of Codex II comes from its
colophon which reads, "The book of Thomas the athlete which
he wrote for the Perfect." The work contains secret sayings
told by Christ to Judas-Thomas, and recorded by Matthias.
Again Thomas is called "twin brother" of Christ. The opening
passage reads, "The secret words spoken by the Savior to Judas
Thomas, and which I have written down, I, Matthew, who
heard them while they spoke together." The time of this revelation was probably between the resurrection and the ascension.

It is possible that this work is identical with the heretical
Gospel of Matthias, a work mentioned by Origen and Eusebius.[12]
However, that gospel may be confused with the *Traditions of
Matthias* cited by Clement of Alexandria and used by the
Nicolaitans and Basilidians. Hippolytus in *Philosopheumena*
said Basilides and his son, Isidore, claimed to have secret dis-
courses they received from Matthias who, in turn, had gotten
them directly from the Lord.

A long discourse of Jesus consisting of Blessings and Woes
(cf. the canonical Gospels) is found in this treatise. From what
little is known of this unpublished text it seems to have stressed
self-knowledge, continency, deliverance from the flesh, and redemption from oblivion. All these are Gnostic motifs, although
some have their counterparts in other religions. For example, it
condemns the flesh, womanhood, and sexuality in typical
Encratite fashion. It promises rest in the kingdom of heaven.
Again, one notes that it is not the individual elements in
Gnosticism which constitute its essence, but their peculiar combination.

---

[11] *Ibid.,* p. 190.
[12] *Ibid.,* p. 226, but Puech disagrees. Cf. *N.T. Apoc.,* I, pp. 308, 312 ff.

*   *   *   *

There are no detailed discussions of the treatises dealt with in this chapter available to date in English. Plumley's forthcoming treatment of the *Hypostasis of the Archons* and Bullard's edition, with translation and commentary, of the same treatise are the only works announced as under preparation.

IX

CODEX V

All of this Codex, except its first treatise, has been edited and published with a German translation.[1] Originally it consisted of eighty-five pages of papyrus. One page of the papyrus was so inferior that it was left blank. The pages vary in size with the largest being about 13 by 24 centimeters (about 5 by 9½ inches). Unfortunately, on most pages of this codex the opening and closing lines are either missing or in fragmentary condition. Apparently a normal page consisted of 28 to 32 lines. Doresse thinks it was written by the same scribe as Codices IV, VI, and VIII.[2] Puech dates the manuscript from the end of the third or the beginning of the fourth century, but this is probably too early.[3]

Our main interest is not in the mechanics of the Codex, but in its fascinating content. It contains five works. The first, *The Epistle of Eugnostos*, is also found in Codex III. This duplication will allow its editors to restore the fragmentary and broken lines of Codex V. The two copies are being edited and published.

Codex V consists of the following works:

1. *The Epistle of Eugnostos*, pp. 1–17
2. *The Apocalypse of Paul*, pp. 17–24.9
3. *The* (first) *Apocalypse of James*, pp. 24.10–44.8
4. *The* (second) *Apocalypse of James*, pp. 44.10–63.32
5. *The Apocalypse of Adam*, pp. 64.1–85.32

---

[1] Alexander Bohlig and Pahor Labib, *Koptisch-gnostische Apokalypsen aus Codex V von Nag Hammadi, Wissenschaftliche Zeitschrift der Martin-Luther Universitat* (Halle-Wittenberg, 1963).

[2] *Secret Books*, pp. 142 f.

[3] *Encyclopedie Francaise*, fasc. 19.42-10, cited in Krause and Labib, *Die Drei Versionen des Apokryphon des Johannes. .* , p. 23.

Evidently pages 86 through 88 were uninscribed. Of these, the last two pages are missing from the extant manuscript.

A. THE EPISTLE OF EUGNOSTOS

Doresse suggests that this work (also found in Codex III) originally may have been the opening part of the untitled Sethian work of Codex II.[4] *Eugnostos* and *The Wisdom of Jesus* (known also from *BG*.[5]) contain exactly the same material, except that in *The Wisdom of Jesus* this material is dissected and rearranged in the form of a dialogue between the disciples and Christ. Fragments of this *Wisdom of Jesus* have been identified by Puech in Papyrus Oxyrhynchus 1081.

The work differs from many Gnostic treatises in that it is a commentary on a prophetic revelation rather than the revelation itself. Eugnostos is also mentioned as transcriber of the *Sacred Book of the Invisible Great Spirit* (*The Gospel of the Egyptians*). His status would seem to be similar to that of the writer of the Qumran Habakkuk *pesher*.

The *Epistle of Eugnostos* opens, like many Gnostic works, with an injunction to rejoice (cf. Ptolemy's *Letter to Flora*). He proceeds to elaborate on the greatness of God who is immortal, ineffable, unknowable, non-created, non-temporal. The ideas here are close to those in the *Apocryphon of John*. The essence of the Supreme Father is intelligence or reasoning.

The *Epistle* differs from the Great Gnostics in its elaboration of the cosmic entities whose number far exceeds the typical scheme of thirty Aeons. However, it does preserve the principle of pairs (syzygy) and male-female (androgyneity). It does not proceed to discuss the creation of the lower world as does the untitled Sethian work of Codex II.[6]

B. THE APOCALYPSE OF PAUL

An *Ascension of Paul* was known to Epiphanius as a Cainite text (*Panarion*, xxxviii.25). However, this work is now lost. It mentioned three heavens instead of the typical Gnostic seven. Another *Apocalypse of St. Paul* was known down to the Middle Ages, being used as a source by Dante in his *Divine Comedy*.

---

[4] *Op. cit.*, p. 195.
[5] Walter Till, *Die gnostischen Schriften des koptischen Papyrus BG.* (TU 60), Akademie Verlag (Berlin, 1955).
[6] The text of the *Epistle* is now being edited. When it is published the present writer hopes to publish a more elaborate treatment of its contents.

With some diversity of details, both these works deal with the same general topic, the ascent to heaven, a topic also found in II Corinthians 12:2.

The Nag Hammadi text, covering less than seven pages of Coptic text, contains very little that is peculiar to the Gnostics. The ascent of the soul is a common Gnostic motif, but even that may come from the Biblical passage cited above. The seven heavens with the cosmic warders is found in several gnostic systems. In Manichaeism these warders are called "customs men," while the Great Gnostics refer to them as Archons, i.e., "rulers." Due to its fantastic embroidery, characteristic of the apocryphal writers of the third and fourth centuries, this work probably should be dated later than the bulk of the Nag Hammadi texts.

The contents can be arranged under eight sections. The first deals with Paul's encounter, as he is on the way to Jericho, with a little boy who asks Paul's name. This little One, however, already knows that Paul is blessed from the womb (Gal. 1:15; cf. Jer. 1:5). He calls upon Paul to awaken his understanding and know the Hidden One in the Revealed.

The second part deals with Paul's ascent to the third and fourth heavens. He is urged on by the voice of the Holy Spirit, "Come, look," etc. This is reminiscent of the passages in Revelation where the voice from heaven speaks at the opening of each of the seven seals. In the third heaven Paul sees the twelve apostles at the right hand and left hand of God. In the fourth heaven he sees the peculiar generation, and angels who resemble God. These angels take a soul, put it in the entrance to the fourth heaven and are flogging it. Then follows a court room interrogation scene.

In section three, at the fifth heaven four angels hold iron staves in their hands. These are used to flog the souls on to judgment. Section four presents Paul in the sixth heaven, beholding a great light. He sees the Customs men. Paul's words before the door, "[Open] to me," seem reminiscent of the formula in the *Descent of Ishtar*. He also sees his fellow apostles in the sixth heaven.

In section five, which deals with the seventh heaven, Paul sees an old man. The old man-little boy-Christ equation is also seen in the *Apocryphon of John*, where it seems to reflect Revelation 1. A lacuna in the text leaves us with no further knowledge of what transpires. The sixth section deals with Paul's entrance into the eighth heaven, called the Ogdoad, wherein he again saw the twelve apostles and greeted them. They all ascended to the ninth heaven, with Paul again greeting its occupants. Finally, in the eighth section, he enters the tenth heaven where Paul greets his fellow spirits.

C. THE (FIRST) APOCALYPSE OF JAMES

This work purports to be a revelation given by the Lord, partly before the passion and partly after the resurrection, to James, His brother, also called James the Righteous. The false equation of James the Righteous with a supposed "twin" of Christ has been anticipated in Codex I, the *Apocryphon of James*, where James the Apostle and James the Lord's brother are confused. Here, however, the Gnostic writer distinctly states that James is not the brother of Jesus "in the material."

Throughout the treatise the familiar dialogue style is maintained. It is a long doctrinal and pastoral conversation between Jesus and James. Jesus is called by James, "Rabbi," indicating the Gnostic stress upon Jesus as a teacher rather than as the Saviour. Although there is passing mention of the passion and resurrection, these events are secondary, not central as in the New Testament. The teaching that James received he was to pass on to Addai.[7] Addai was to inscribe them after ten years.

The work occupies over twenty pages of text. Unfortunately about eight lines at the bottom of the first thirteen pages are badly preserved, and the last seven pages are in very poor condition, thereby making reconstruction and translation of over half of each of these pages uncertain or impossible. The fragmentary colophon at the end has been glossed above the first two lines of text, reading "The Apocalypse of James." While the language of the text is basically Sahidic, there are frequent uses of Sub-Achmimic forms and at least one occurrence of a Fayyumic variant.

Two points of contact with the *Gospel of the Egyptians* (a different work than the Nag Hammadi text of that title) seem evident. As in the *Apocalypse*, so in *Egyptians*, James is given an exalted position alongside the supernatural powers who have charge of the great Baptisms (according to Doresse).[8] According to Clement of Alexandria (*Stromata* iii.13.92) Salome is addressed in a passage in *Egyptians*; the same words are spoken about Mariam in *Thomas* (Saying No. 114), and are paralleled in the *Apocalpyse of James* 41.16-18.

The relationship between this *Apocalypse* and the unpublished

---

[7]Cf. Bohlig's note, *op. cit.*, p. 46.
[8]*Op. cit.*, p. 237.

Apocryphon or *Epistle of James* of Codex I remains unclear. In the latter, 550 days after the resurrection Jesus appears to Peter and James to instruct them. Furthermore, the *Epistle of James* is not definitely Gnostic, but only vague enough so that it could be used for Gnostic purposes. In contrast, the first *Apocalypse of James* seems definitely Gnostic. Bohlig has singled out four Gnostic motifs as evidence of this: (1) the Ascent of the Soul, (2) the Doctrine of Fate, (3) the Sophia and Achamoth (lower Sophia), and (4) the Doctrine of the Paraclete.[9] Numerous close ties with Valentinian doctrine lead Bohlig to believe that the work came from that source.[10] However, there are also some ties with the *Apocryphon of John,* and with Naasene teaching, while the mention of "customs men" reminds one of Manichaeism.

Mention has been made of parallels with *Thomas.* The *Apocalypse* says (41.15-19), "The Changeable went up to the Unchangeable, And the work of the Female came to the work of this Manhood." This idea of the restoration of a primeval androgyneity is expressed in *Thomas* (Saying No. 114) as follows: "Jesus said [of Mariam]: 'Lo, I shall lead her so that I shall make her a male, in order that she, herself, may become a living spirit, being like you males, because every woman who shall make herself a male shall enter into the kingdom of heaven'" (cf. Saying No. 22). A similar idea is found in II Clement 12:2.[11] Clement of Alexandria (*Stromata,* iii.9.63) says the Gnostics taught that Jesus said, "I have come to release the work of the female."

Another point at which the *Apocalypse of James* shows affinity to *Thomas* concerns the authorship of the *Apocalypse.* In Saying No. 12 when the disciples ask who shall be great over them after the departure of Jesus, the Saviour tells them: "In that place to which you have come, you shall go to James the Righteous, this one because of whom the heaven and the earth came into existence." The prominence of James is also attested in Clement's *Hypotyposes* (as preserved in Eusebius' *Eccl. Hist.* II.1.4-5), where after the resurrection Christ reveals Himself to James, "who was one of those who are regarded as brothers of the Lord." Then Jesus "passed on Gnosis to James the Just, to John, and to Peter, who themselves (passed it on) to

---

[9]*Op. cit.,* p. 27.
[10]*Ibid.* Cf. the inclusion of the *Epistle of James* in Codex I, which is otherwise completely Valentinian.
[11]"When the two shall become one, and the outer as the inner and the manly with the womanly neither male nor female."

the other apostles, the other apostles to the Seven, among whom
Barnabas was included. . . ."[12]

The *Gospel of Hebrews* also regarded James as the Lord's
brother. In Jerome's *Commentary on Micah* (7:7), James was
the first person to see the risen Christ (*contra* I Cor. 15:7), and
was then converted.

Bohlig outlines the contents of the first *Apocalypse of James*
as follows:

1. Dialogue before the passion, 24.10–30.11
2. James — from Jesus' departure to His reappearance, 30.11–
   31.1
3. Dialogue after the resurrection of Jesus, 31.2–42.19
4. Confession and martyrdom of James, 42.20–44.6

D. The (Second) Apocalypse of James

The (second) *Apocalypse of James,* composed of twenty
pages of Coptic text, is reputedly a speech of James the Just
(Righteous) given in Jerusalem, and then recorded by Mareim,
a priest. The speech was delivered on the fifth step of the
temple, probably the uppermost of the last five steps (cf. *Ps.
Clem. Recognitions* i.66.70.73). It would seem that the immediate addressee of his speech is Theuda, his father (*sic*), perhaps to be equated with Jude of Luke 6:16 and Acts 1:13
(passages where the text is elliptic), although a multitude is
present to hear the speech.

This *Apocalypse* contains a number of references, or allusions
to, or perhaps more correctly, echoes of the canonical Scriptures.
Books thus represented include John, Matthew, Colossians,
Galatians, and especially Isaiah. The work is not so clearly
Gnostic as the *Apocryphon of John,* or the *Gospel of Truth.*
However, there is enough Gnostic terminology definitely to
credit the work to a Gnostic circle. Typical terms such as "The
Unchangeable," "the Pleroma," "Aeon," "the All," and "Stranger"
appear in the work.

James is certainly to be identified with the Biblical James,
the traditional first bishop of the Jerusalem church. As in the
New Testament Epistle of James, he is the Lord's brother.
Significantly, in this *Apocalypse* he is said to be his "milk-
brother," that is, he was suckled by the same mother.

---

[12]Doresse, *op. cit.,* p. 236. Cf. Bohlig, *op. cit.,* p. 27.

Unfortunately, since the opening and closing lines of most pages are completely lost or in fragmentary condition, it is difficult to follow the thought throughout the work. However, enough is clear to enable Bohlig to suggest the following outline of its contents:[13]

1. Introductory action, pp. 44.1–45, end or 46, beginning
2. The Speech of James in which he introduces himself, pp. 46–49, end
3. The Greeting scene, pp. 50.5–50, end
4. Speech of Jesus, pp. 51–57.11. (In this section there are sayings about the Father, a passage giving his negative attributes as in the *Gospel of Truth* and *A.J.* Great stress is put upon James as a Redeemer — to be understood in the Gnostic sense that he imparts knowledge that saves. He is the Illuminator.)
5. Farewell scene, pp. 57.12–57.19
6. The Speech of James before the Judge, pp. 57.20–60.26. (This includes a Hymn to Jesus and other poetical passages.)
7. The Martyrdom of James, pp. 60.28–63.30

The work ends with the multitude casting James down from the cornerstone of the temple and stoning him. James utters a Psalm of Trust as he is put to death. This whole scene is reminiscent of the death of the first Christian martyr, Stephen.

The carefully thought out plan of the treatise is evident in that it contains three speeches sandwiched between four brief action scenes.

E.   APOCALYPSE OF ADAM

For some reason, the Biblical figure of Adam has had a strange fascination for writers of apocryphal and apocalyptic literature. The writers of Gnostic texts are no exception to this attraction. The *Apocalypse of Adam* is used as the vehicle for a purported revelation given to Adam, then in turn passed on by him to his son, Seth. The exact relationship of this Nag Hammadi work to other apocryphal literature dealing with Adam is as yet undefined. The heresiologist, Epiphanius (*Panarion*, xxvi. 8.1), speaks of the Great Gnostics using a work called *The Revelation of Adam*. Bohlig thinks that this may refer to a work identical with or similar to the *Apocalypse of Adam*.[14] John of

---

[13]*Op. cit.*, p. 57.
[14]*Op. cit.*, p. 86. The article by George W. MacRae, "The Coptic-Gnostic Apocalypse of Adam," *The Heythrop Journal*, VI (1965), pp. 31-35, came to the author's attention too late to be used in this discussion.

Parallos, a sixth-century bishop in Lower Egypt, denounced the so-called *Teachings of Adam*. There also is an apocryphal *Book of Adam* that was translated from the Ethiopic into German in 1853, and into English in 1882. This *Book of Adam*, probably identical with the *Apocalypse of Moses*, is a work different from the Nag Hammadi text. The Latin *Life of Adam and Eve* contains an apocalyptic vision related by Adam to Seth and has a motif common to the *Apocalypse of Paul* in this Codex.[15]

That Adam and Seth were primary figures in gnostic thought is very evident from a cursory examination of the literature handed down to us. Bohlig lists at least eight Sethian works (seven from the Nag Hammadi corpus): The *Apocalypse of Adam,* the *Gospel of the Egyptians,* the *Apocalypse of Dositheus,* the *Second Speech of the Great Seth,* the *Book of the Strangers* (*Allogenes*), the *Apocalypse of Zostrianos,* the *Apocryphon of John,* and the untitled old Gnostic work of Codex Bruce.[16] The *Apocryphon of John* evidently stems from a different Gnostic sect than the other texts. However, it seems likely that the *Apocalypse of Adam* comes from the circle of Gnostics called "Sethian," as do the other texts enumerated. The Barbelo-gnostics, as represented by the *Apocryphon of John,* were closely related to, but not identical with, the Sethians.

Further evidence of the attraction of Adam and Seth in the wider world of related Gnostic groups is abundant. The Syrian *Chronicle* (*ca.* A.D. 775) from a monastery at Zuqnin, spoke of Adam giving revelations to Seth.[17] The Manichaeans had a *Book of Mysteries* in their *Kephalia* (ch. X) that was devoted to Adam's testimony regarding the future advent of Christ. The Mandaeans believed Adam was the first recipient of secret books, and that their own book, the *Ginza,* was one of those books. Their mythology had several points in common with the content of the *Apocalypse of Adam,* including the personage Sithil.

The *Apocalypse of Adam* occupies twenty-two pages of fairly well-preserved text. The bottoms of most pages are fragmentary, thereby presenting some problems in following the chain of thought. However, in the main, the ideas can be discerned and followed throughout. The language is clear, with only a few dialectical or syntactical peculiarities, these implying another site than Nag Hammadi as the place where the text was actually translated from Greek into Coptic.

---

[15]Bohlig, *op. cit.,* p. 16.
[16]*Op. cit.,* p. 87 n.
[17]An excerpt is given in Doresse, *op. cit.,* p. 185. He has an extended discussion of the Adam literature.

The work purports to be a revelation by Adam, about one hundred years before his death, to his son, Seth, when Seth was seven hundred years old. Seth stands out as salvation-bringer, which is his typical Gnostic, representative role.

In addition to the introduction and conclusion, the work has two main divisions: (1) Adam's account of the experiences of himself and Eve, and (2) the *Apocalypse*, proper, composing the bulk of the text. In this section four main themes are presented: (a) The flood and the preservation of the seed of Seth. Noah is equated with Deucalion, and is saved by a literal ark, *contra* the *Apocryphon of John*. (b) The destruction of some of Seth's seed by fire, and the preservation of certain men from the Demiurge. (c) The coming of the Illuminator (Phoster) to redeem Noah's sons. This passage includes the thirteen sayings by the various royalties (kingdoms), and another by the unroyal generation, about the origins of Phoster. (d) The penitence of the people and the sentence of judgment.

From a survey of the content of this work Bohlig comes to some conclusions concerning its origin.[18] He says it must be a Syro-Palestinian production, probably from a baptizing sect, but is pre-Christian. He calls attention to the Iranian, Hellenistic, Jewish, and Gnostic elements. Bohlig thinks it comes from a Sethian circle at second-hand. Among the relationships he notes are those to *Jubilees*, the Mandaean *Ginza*, and the Manichaean *Homilies*. Doresse thinks the content of the *Apocalypse of Adam* goes back to the Persian *Avesta*. The successive royalties in the *Apocalypse* are also in Zoroastrianism.[19] These speculations are syncretized in the *Book of the Cave of Treasures*. The Biblical allusions are practically all Old Testament, with one possible reference to Romans 1:21 and another to Revelation 12:6.

This *Apocalypse* seems to be a typically Sethian Gnostic production, revealing some of the relationship of ideas between the Great Gnostics, the Mandaeans, and the Manichaeans. It shows the pre-gnostic Iranian, Jewish, and Hellenistic sources which were syncretized in Gnosticism. In the syncretism, *gnosis* (knowledge) stands forth as the means of salvation.

---

[18]*Op. cit.*, p. 95.
[19]Cf. Doresse, *op. cit.*, p. 184 and ref. to Bidez-Cumont there.

X

GNOSTICISM AND BIBLICAL STUDIES

Some hints of the importance of the Nag Hammadi texts to the Biblical student have been given throughout this work. There remains the task of gathering together these various hints and elaborating upon the vast importance of this find so fortuitously made by the Egyptian peasants. Perhaps this can best be done by treating the material under four categories: (1) The Canon of the New Testament, (2) Textual History, (3) Biblical Theology or Interpretation, and (4) Developments within modern theology.

A. The Canon of the New Testament

Under this rubric a number of related ideas should be discussed. Because the Gnostics claimed to possess authentic gospels, acts, epistles, and apocalypses, the church of the second century was forced to decide what was to be accepted and what was to be rejected. This process culminated in the "formal" canons of Laodicea (A.D. 363), Carthage (A.D. 397), and Hippo (A.D. 419). However, these were not the first lists of "accepted" books. They were merely formal statements of what the consensus of opinion had been in the "great" church, possibly as early as A.D. 140. The very production of false gospels, etc., indicates the prior acceptance of those that were true. The Biblical works were early accepted as authentic and inspired, therefore the Gnostics hoped to get their works accepted by mimicking the Biblical works. Counterfeit money always testifies to the acceptance of genuine.

While the Gnostic movement was compelling the church formally to declare what was canonical, it was also, unintentionally, giving its own testimony as to what was accepted in Christian circles in the mid-second century A.D. The Nag Hammadi texts directly or indirectly cite most of the New Testament books, and borrow from some of them repeatedly.

This necessitates reckoning with the possibility that the New
Testament canon was completed and accepted much earlier
than has commonly been supposed.[1] Here it is necessary only
to point out that both the *Gospel of Truth* and the *Gospel of
Philip* know and recognize the greater part of the New Testament as authoritative. The *Apocryphon of John* alludes to or
cites a great number of New Testament books. Some of these
citations and allusions will be examined in the discussion of
such special problems as the Johannine literature, Hebrews, and
II Peter.

The Nag Hammadi texts shed light on some of the problems
concerning authorship and date of certain New Testament
books — problems of vital importance in deciding upon canonicity. The first of these, in Biblical order, has to do with John's
Gospel. However, that question cannot be discussed apart from
the question of the authorship of Revelation. The disjunctive
canon of Dionysius of Alexandria (*ca.* A.D. 200) that the two
books cannot come from the same author is widely held today.
In connection with the Gospel, the evidence of the Nag Hammadi texts indicates two things: first, that the Gospel cannot
possibly be dated in the second century since it was already
widely quoted as canonical by A.D. 140[2] (the John Rylands
fragment had earlier given manuscript evidence favoring the
traditional date of *ca.* A.D. 95). Second, the Nag Hammadi
texts, along with those from Qumran, make it impossible to
regard the Gospel of John as a Hellenistically informed Gospel.
It is clearly from a Syro-Palestinian milieu, with typical Jewish
background.[3] This latter fact should have a profound bearing
on recent attempts to interpret the Gospel as viewed through

---

[1]Cf. Puech, *New Testament Apocrypha,* I, pp. 240 f. (He says concerning *E.V.*:
"Moreover the numerous and diverse Biblical citations would make the work
a very valuable witness for the state of the New Testament canon at that
date.") Cf. also Wilson, *The Gospel of Philip,* p. 191; and van Unnik,
The Jung Codex, pp. 122-25 for further details.

[2]Two Nag Hammadi texts from the second century used the Gospel of John
extensively. Note the following parallels from *E.V.*: 18.8 with John 16:3;
22.21 with John 10:4; 26.7 with John 1:14; 30.34 with John 20:22 (where
the Western text has the added phrase "on them"); 37.21 with John 1:3.
In *A.J.* note 47.11 f. with John 3:13; 51.15 ff. with John 1:18; 55.17 with
John 1:14, 18; 70.32 with John 1:5; 80.6 with John 20:31. Wilson lists
thirteen sayings in the *Gospel of Philip* that have some relationship to
passages in the Gospel of John.

[3]Cf. William Foxwell Albright, "Recent Discoveries in Palestine and the Gospel
of St. John," *The New Testament Background and Its Eschatology* (ed. W.
D. Davies and David Daube) (Cambridge, 1956), pp. 153-171, for a
fuller discussion.

Gnostic spectacles. John does not borrow from the Gnostics, but the Gnostics from John.

The related problem of the authorship of Revelation is illuminated by the *Apocryphon of John,* which opens with a revelatory scene highly reminiscent of and dependent upon the first chapter of the Biblical work. In this opening scene when the Saviour appears to John, He speaks the words of Revelation 1:19 almost verbatim. All this occurs in the context where the author of the Gnostic *Apocryphon* claims to be John, "the brother of James, these who are the sons of Zebedee." Evidently, the mid-second century Gnostics felt sure that John the Apostle wrote the Biblical Book of Revelation.[4] It seems quite certain the doubts as to the authenticity (and canonicity) of Revelation were not part of the early post-Apostolic period, but developed toward the end of the second century under the impact of abuses in the Montanist movement.

Perhaps the biggest puzzle in the New Testament is the question of who wrote the Epistle to the Hebrews. The fact that its authorship could not be settled weighed heavily in the arguments against its canonicity. Now the Nag Hammadi texts show that by A.D. 140 the Epistle was widely used by both the Western and Eastern branches of the church. Such wide usage is attested in the *Gospel of Truth,* the *Gospel of Philip,* and the *Apocryphon of John.*[5] Its early acceptance throws the burden of proof upon those who, in the second and third century, wanted to reject that Epistle.

One of the most generally accepted "conclusions" of modern critical study of the New Testament is the late date (second century) for II Peter. This conclusion probably will need to take into account the data from the Nag Hammadi texts. These texts, specifically the *Gospel of Truth* and the *Apocryphon of*

---

[4]Cf. Andrew Helmbold, "A Note on the Authorship of the Apocalypse," *New Testament Studies,* VIII (1961), pp. 77-79.

[5]In *E.V.* cf. 19.13-17 with Hebrews 8:11; 19.35 f. with Hebrews 8:10; 20.10 with Hebrews 2:17 (the only place where "merciful and faithful" are coupled in the New Testament); 26.2 with Hebrews 4:12; 38.10 with Hebrews 1:5; 5:5. In *A.J.* cf. 75.24-28 with Hebrews 12:16-17; 75.22 f. with Hebrews 10:26-27, 39; 78.2 f. with Hebrews 4:9. An allusion to Hebrews 12:18 may be found in *A.J.* 47.33. In the *Gospel of Philip* the following citations from or allusions to Hebrews may be seen: Saying No. 82 and Hebrews 4:11; Saying No. 76 and Hebrews 9:2 ff.; Saying No. 125 and Hebrews 6:19-20; 10:20. Some think *Philip* is specifically Valentinian. If so, that fact would indicate that its author and the author of *E.V.* (both representing Western or Roman Gnosticism) provide a second-century witness from the Western church for the authenticity of Hebrews. Additional instances of the use of Hebrews by *E.V.* can be seen in the work by Soren Giversen cited in the bibliography.

John, use quotations and/or allusions to this disputed epistle.[6] Of course, it is always possible to argue that the Gnostics borrowed from a common source which the pseudonymous author of the epistle used. However, such reasoning seems specious when the real reason for rejecting II Peter appears to be theological rather than factual. The "good" reason for rejecting Petrine authorship, i.e., there is no early witness to the book, is partially removed by the use of II Peter in the Nag Hammadi texts.

While speculation is useless, the publication of the remaining works from Nag Hammadi will undoubtedly throw additional light upon these and other questions about the authenticity, authorship, and canonicity of New Testament books. The *Gospel of the Egyptians,* the *Book of Thomas the Athlete,* the *Acts of Peter,* and the *Apocalypse of Peter* should be especially helpful at this point.

B. The History of the Text and Source Criticism

These two related fields — the former dealing with isolated words and phrases, the latter dealing with whole blocks of material — are both affected by the finds at Nag Hammadi. Again, it is too early to provide dogmatic answers, but the evidence can be pointed out. The *Gospel of Thomas* and the *Gospel of Philip* both contain a number of passages that deviate from the *textus receptus.* These deviations quite frequently are in agreement with the so-called "Western" text of the New Testament.[7] This text, or preferably, textual family, includes such works as Codex Beza (D), the Old Latin and Old Syriac

---

[6]*A.J.* 72.8 reads: "clothed them with a blackness of darkness." *A.J.* 75.24-31 says: "those who knew [*gnosis*]and withdrew" shall suffer this fate: "The place wherein the poverty angels shall go, they shall be received there, the place of non-repentance. And they shall be guarded to the day when they shall torture those who had blasphemed against the Spirit." *A.J.* 77.3 makes reference to Noah's preaching to the sons of men. When these passages are grouped and compared to II Peter 2:4-5, it seems likely that the author of *A.J.* knew II Peter. The evidence from *E.V.* is more ambiguous; cf. *E.V.* 18.19 with II Peter 2:2, and *E.V.* 30.27 with II Peter 1:17.

[7]Deviations in *Philip* include 130.17 agreeing with Matthew 9:15 in Codex Beza and Latin; 132.27 f. agreeing with Matthew 23:38 in Beza, Latin, and Clement; 111.26 reads "seventy-two" instead of the usual seventy, a variation of Luke 10:1, 17 found also in Beza, Syriac, Cureton Syr. In *Thomas* Logia 91 shows the author knew Matthew 16:1-4 with Western interpolations. *E.V.* adds the phrase "on them" to John 20:22, an addition also in the Western text (*E.V.* 30.34). *E.V.* 37.21 approximates Matthew 10:29, saying that nothing happens "apart from the Will of the Father." This variant occurs in several Old Latin manuscripts. *E.V.* 38.10 has an allusion to Luke 3:32 that follows a reading found in Beza.

Versions, and most Ante-Nicene Fathers. The common theory
is that the "Western" text originated in the Syrian church, a fact
that ties in well with linguistic and thematic evidence from the
Gospel of Thomas and the *Gospel of Philip.* Just what bearing
the Nag Hammadi usage will have on current New Testament
critical studies remains to be seen. At any rate it will have a
bearing upon the study of the Nag Hammadi texts themselves,
for it makes clear their origin in the Syro-Palestinian environ-
ment.[8] This, in turn, argues for a Jewish-Christian background
for the origin of the "great Gnostics." Thus the early belief that
Gnosticism went back to Simon Magus may not be far amiss.

Probably more important than their contributions to the sci-
ence of textual criticism is the light the Nag Hammadi texts
shed on the problems of Gospel sources. Much modern study of
the Gospels is occupied with the *sitz im leben* of particular
pericopae, the cultural and cultic situation in which a given
story, saying, miracle, etc. was first told. Since the *Gospel of
Thomas* and the *Gospel of Philip* offer so little historical setting
for their "sayings," apparently they would have nothing to
offer at this point. However, a careful study of the canonical
sayings and incidents recorded in the Gnostic texts, and their
agreement or disagreement with the Biblical parallels, should
yield some fruit. Are the Gnostic gospels dependent upon the
canonical Gospels; do they both borrow from a common source;
do they go back to different sources; or is it even possible that
the canonical writers borrowed from Gnostic sources? These
questions vex students of the Nag Hammadi texts, and will soon
demand the attention of all students of Gospel traditions. The
answers given have been nearly as varied as the questions, so
further study must occur before dogmatic conclusions can be
reached.[9]

C. Biblical Interpretation

The first area of concern to modern Biblical scholars is the
Gnostic interpretation of Scripture as demonstrated in their
texts. Many Nag Hammadi texts are more anti-Judaistic than
such New Testament books as the Gospel of John and Galatians.

---

[8]For further discussion cf. Robert McL. Wilson, "Gnostic Origins," *V.C.,* IX
    (1955), pp. 193-211, and "Gnostic Origins Again," *V.C.,* XI (1957), pp.
    93-110.
[9]Cf. the discussions in Grant-Freedman, Turner and Montefiore, and the *Jung
    Codex.* More recently reference to neglect of the Nag Hammadi evidence
    has been pointed up in Richard Longenecker's review of *Paul and James* by
    Walter Schmithals, in *B.E.T.S.,* VIII (1965), pp. 175-176.

There are anti-Pharisaic attitudes in the *Apocryphon of John* and the *Hypostasis of the Archons*. The anti-Jahwistic, anti-Old Testament attitude of the *Apocryphon of John* and the *Gospel of Thomas* (cf. Logia 52 and 53) is typically Gnostic. However, this attitude of the Gnostics was well known before the discovery at Chenoboskion. What new factor does the find add to the understanding of Gnostic hermeneutics? Attention should be called to the eisegesis, or "demythologization" of Old Testament passages that is especially prominent in the *Apocryphon of John*. Several times the author says, "It is not as Moses (the Pentateuch) said." Then follows the Gnostic re-interpretation of the text. This re-interpretation de-literalizes, de-historicizes the event. For example, Noah's ark is not an ark, but a cloud of light. In the understanding of modern Biblical interpretation, the Nag Hammadi texts should warn scholars of the dangers involved in any interpretation that is not based on sound historico-grammatical exegesis.[10] Modern attempts at demythologization might take caution at this point. It is strange that those who accuse New Testament writers of being influenced by Gnostic ideas have themselves fallen prey to Gnostic methodology in Biblical interpretation.

The second area of concern is the effect of Gnostic systems of interpretation upon the early church. Stated simply, Gnostic interpretation (with its resultant Gnostic "theology") forced the church carefully to define two things: who or what was the true church, i.e., the body whose interpretation was to be considered normative; and what did that church accept as the essence of the teaching of Scripture. Actually these two things overlap, for the church defined itself as that body which had the true succession of bishops and the true faith. This true faith was then expressed in a semi-formal way and, under the impact of later controversies, came to full expression in such formal creeds as those of Nicea and Chalcedon. However, the basic doctrines of those creeds had already been clearly defined during the second century upon the basis of early confessional statements that some believe were present in the Scripture. Already by the time of Tertullian (*ca.* A.D. 225) he could speak of the "Church of the Authentic Rule of Faith" (*Adv. Valentinianos*, 4).

---

[10]Robert M. Grant, "Two Gnostic Gospels," *J.B.L.*, LXXIX (1960), p. 8, says Valentinian exegesis "shows the dangers of allegorization without the controls provided either by common sense or by some dogmatic system with roots on earth."

D. Modern Theology

The past is useful only as it helps in understanding the present. The manner in which the Gnostics and the Great Church interpreted Scripture and formulated their theologies in the second century is of interest only as today it helps evaluate Scripture interpretation (and misinterpretation). It is a common truism that there are very few (if any) really new problems in exegesis and theology. There are only new slants on old problems. So modern theology grapples with age-old questions, seeking answers that will "speak to the condition" of a "world come of age." The responsibility of the Biblical student is to hold up these modern answers to the searching light of Biblical exegesis to see if they accord with God's revelation in His Word — the written Word and the Living Word. At this point the Nag Hammadi texts can be helpful. If Gnostic answers to perennial problems were rejected as un-Biblical (and unworkable) in the second century, what guarantee is there that similar or identical answers given by twentieth-century theologians are not just as un-Biblical (and unworkable)?[11] Some themes of modern theology are not really modern for they are present in the Gnostic texts.

One of these themes is presented on the opening pages of the *Apocryphon of John,* in the *Gospel of Truth,* and at other places in the Nag Hammadi corpus. This is the motif that the real God is essentially unknowable to man. He is the ineffable, who can be described only in the terms of what He is not. In the twentieth century the expression used is that "God is totally other." If God is that ineffable, why attempt to get acquainted? The Gnostics sought to remove God from this earth for different reasons than those of twentieth century Neo-orthodoxy, but the net result is the same — a God who is too remote to be of much help to modern man facing the complexity and the demonic in modern civilization. The Great Church rejected the Gnostic interpretation of God in favor of the more Biblical and more appealing view that God is concerned with man day-by-day as illustrated in Jesus' famous remark about the fall of the sparrow.

Another motif common to Gnostics in the second century and some theologians in the twentieth is that of salvation via esoteric knowledge. Simple Bible stories about Jesus, a literal

---

[11]Hans Jonas, *The Gnostic Religion* (2nd ed.) (Boston: Beacon Press, 1963), has an Epilogue entitled "Gnosticism, Existentialism, and Nihilism" (pp. 320-340), which deals with some of the implications for modern theology.

cross, and a real resurrection may be sufficient for common people, ordinary churchmen. However, the really spiritual person goes beyond this to see cross, resurrection, ascension, Pentecost, etc. merely as symbols of higher truths. To be sure, even the ordinary churchman recognizes the cross as a demonstration of God's redeeming love. In contrast, some modern interpreters go beyond this in seeing meanings too mysterious for all but highly trained philosopher-exegetes to understand. Therefore, the true Christian can only be the Gnostic — the one who knows all these secret doctrines. The ordinary churchman is only a semi-Christian — the "psychic" as compared to the "pneumatic" in the Gnostic systems.

A third motif of Gnosticism is that of moral or immoral conduct. Starting with the basic premise that matter is evil (and the body is matter), the Gnostics arrived at two different conclusions. Some Gnostics said that since the body was of this world it made no difference what one did with it; therefore they became antinomian libertines. Others said that the body, being matter and evil, was to be negated. These Gnostics became ascetics of the strictest type. Modern theology has little to offer along the lines of this second group, but it does have some parallels to the first group. The so-called "new morality," by changing the locus of right or wrong from an external standard applied to the material body to an internal standard applied to the mind, follows the lead of the Gnostics who, by their actions, said that right or wrong was "all in your mind."

Finally, the Gnostic habit of using Christian terminology to express what was basically an un-Christian philosophy should serve as a warning to the twentieth century that all who speak with the vocabulary of the church may not be uttering the message of the church. Since many current theologies have so vitiated the meaning of traditional theological words, there is danger that the use of sound terminology will be equated with sound theology. The Gnostics used terms such as redemption, sealing, cross, anointing, rest, etc., but meant something far different from what orthodox Christians meant when they used the same words. These and many other helpful insights accrue by the recovery of the Nag Hammadi texts from the sands of Egypt. Puech is quite right when he applies to the recovery of these texts the words of Exodus 7:3: "I will multiply my signs and wonders in the land of Egypt."[12]

---

[12]*Jung Codex*, p. 34.

SELECTED BIBLIOGRAPHY

Barrett, C. K. "The Terminology of *E.V.* and the Gospel of John," in *Current Issues in New Testament Interpretation,* ed. William Klassen and Graydon F. Snyder. New York: Harper and Row, 1962, pp. 224-238.

Giversen, Soren. "The Apocryphon of John and Genesis," *Studia Theologica,* XVII (1963), pp. 60-76.

Helmbold, Andrew K. "A Note on the Authorship of the Apocalypse," *New Testament Studies,* VIII (1961), pp. 77-79.

Quispel, Gilles. "Gnosticism and the New Testament," *V.C.,* XIX (1965), pp. 65-85.

————————. "Some Remarks on the Gospel of Thomas," *New Testament Studies,* V (1959), pp. 276-290.

Wilson, Robert McL. "Thomas and the Growth of the Gospel," *Harvard Theological Review,* LIII (1960), pp. 231-250.

————————. "Thomas and the Synoptic Gospels," *Expository Times,* LXXII (1960), pp. 36-39.

GLOSSARY

Technical and Gnostic terms not defined in the body of this work

Aeon: One of the pre-temporal beings forming the Gnostic Pleroma; *or* one of the sons or powers created by the Demiurge; *or* an age or indefinite period.

agrapha: A saying of Jesus not recorded in the canonical Gospels.

apocalypse: A revelation of doctrinal import, frequently involving future events, and often attributed to a great person of the past, e.g., *The Apocalypse of Adam.*

apocrypha: A book of doubtful authority not admitted to the canon of Holy Scripture.

apocryphon: A secret book, or a secret revelation, to be shared with initiates only, e.g., *The Apocryphon of John.*

Archon: One of the world rulers or planetary spirits; frequently believed to be associated with the twelve signs of the Zodiac.

Basilidians: followers of the Gnostic, Basilides of Alexandria (117-161). They taught that there were two self-existent principles, and that the world was a result of development from below rather than an outgrowth of the emanations from above.

Cainites: An Ophitic sect which worshiped Cain. They are supposed to have believed that Judas Iscariot best perceived truth.

Carpocratians: The followers of the Gnostic, Carpocrates. Strong in first half of second century, A.D. Their belief was a mixture of Platonism and Christianity, teaching that the world was created by angels, and that souls experienced transmigration.

Cerinthians: Followers of the Christian heretic, Cerinthus (*ca.* A.D. 100). They believed matter was evil; the world was created by a Demiurge. Jesus was a mere man who received the divine Christ at baptism, and became mere man again before the crucifixion.

Chrism: A Gnostic sacrament of anointing (*with oil*).

97

colophon: An inscription giving the title and/or author found at the end of a treatise.

Decad: A group of ten Aeons, the first five pairs or syzygies in the Pleroma of the Barbelo-gnostics.

Demiurge: The creator God of the Gnostics, the God of the Old Testament; frequently called Yaldabaoth, Samael, or Saclas.

emanation: One of the thirty Aeons composing the Pleroma; each Aeon being conceived of as a ray coming forth from the Supreme Deity.

Encratites: A heretical movement stressing strict discipline or asceticism. Possibly Tatian was an Encratite. Some of them had Gnostic or docetic leanings. . .

Ennead: A group of nine Aeons of the Pleroma; with their consorts would comprise the first two stages of the Pleroma, i.e., the Ogdoad plus a Decad.

Eucharist: A Christian and Gnostic sacrament, literally "thanksgiving." Probably the Gnostic rite was close to the orthodox Christian mass or Lord's Supper.

hamartiology: The doctrine of human sin.

Hermetics: A religious group of the period between first and fourth centuries, A.D. Grew out of fusion of worship of Hermes and Toth, along with Platonic philosophy and Oriental speculation. Most famous literary remains of the movement is *Hermes Trismegistos.* Had some affinities with Gnosticism.

Mandaeans: A baptizing sect of Mesopotamia believed to have originated in Palestine. Flourished from second to eighth centuries, but still survives. Has many affinities with the Great Gnostics.

Manichaeans: A semi-gnostic ascetic sect founded by Mani (b. A.D. 215), who claimed to be the last of a series of prophets including Zoroaster and Christ. The system is based on Persian dualism. Survived into medieval times in several semi-Christian groups.

Marcionites: The followers of Marcion (*ca.* A.D. 144), one of the earliest Gnostic groups. Believed in two gods: one just (Jahweh) and one good (the real God). Rejected O.T., practiced asceticism.

Montanists: A Christian sect that flourished in the last half of the second century, A.D. It stressed the role of the Holy Spirit, ecstatic prophecy, and the imminent return of Christ.

Ogdoad: The first eight Aeons in the Gnostic Pleroma.

Pleroma: The thirty Aeons composing the totality of the Supreme Being's attributes; the beings who exist beyond the world of sense.

Simonians: The Gnostic sect named for Simon Magus. In this system Simon is the highest power (i.e., God). His consort is Helen of Tyre, a prostitute who is the mother of all, including the angels who create the world.

syzygy: A pair of Aeons in the Pleroma, male and female counterparts.

INDEX OF SUBJECTS

Abel, 53, 74
Achamoth (see Echamoth), 83
Acts of Peter, 17, 45, 91
Acts of Thomas, 55, 60
Adam, 51, 52, 53, 68f., 73, 85, 86, 87
Addai, 82
Aeons, 26, 29, 43, 50, 69, 80, 84, 97
agrapha, 21, 58, 97
Albigenses, 31
Albright, William F., 89n.
Allogenes Supreme, 17
angels, 51, 52, 53
apocalypse, 97
Apocalypse of Adam, 16, 48n., 79, 85-87
Apocalypse of Dositheus, 17, 86
Apocalypse of James (first), 16, 48n., 79, 82-84
Apocalypse of James (second), 16, 48n., 79, 84f.
Apocalypse of Moses, 86
Apocalypse of Paul, 16, 48n., 79, 80-82
Apocalypse of Peter, 17, 91
Apocalypse of Zostrianos, 86
apocryphon, 97
Apocryphon of John, 15, 16, 19, 20, 25n., 26, 27, 29, 30, 37, 42, 45-53, 66, 69, 73, 74, 75, 76, 80, 81, 83, 84, 85, 86, 87, 89, 90, 93
Archons, 28, 50, 51, 52, 73, 74f., 81, 97
Archangelike of Moses the Prophet, 76
Ariel, 76
Arimanios, 46, 49

Ascension of Isaiah, 34
ascent of the soul, 27f., 81, 83
Asclepius, 17
Atargates, 29n.
Audians, 30
Augustine, 61
Authentic Discourse of Hermes, 17
Avesta, 87

baptism, 69f., 82
Barbelo, 29, 50
Barbelo-gnostics, 25, 27, 29, 30, 40, 46, 66, 86
Barclay, Wm., 44n.
Barnabas, 84
Barrett, C.K., 96
Bartholomew, 66
Basilides, Basilidians, 61, 77, 97
Baynes, Charlotte, 27
Bogomils, 31
Bohlig, Alex., 72n., 79n., 83, 84, 85, 86, 87
Book of Adam, 86
Book of the Cave of Treasures, 87
Book of Jeu, 24
Book of Norea, 16, 72f., 75, 76
Book of Strangers, 17, 86
Book of Thomas the Athlete, 16, 60, 72, 77, 91
Book of Zoroaster, (17), 46, 52, 86
Bridal Chamber, 68ff.
Bullard, Roger A., 72n., 78
Burkitt, Francis C., 23n., 31

Cain, 53, 74
Cainites, 80, 97

31352

canon, 30, 43, 68, 88-91
Carpocratians 29, 96
Cathari, 31
Cerfaux, L. and Garitte, G., 20n.
Cerinthians, 29, 97
Chrism, 69f., 97
Christ, 34, 49, 50, 57, 70, 80, 83, 86
Chronicle of Zuknun, 86
Clement of Alexandria, 24, 43n., 61, 67, 70, 77, 82, 83
Codex Berolinensis 8502, 15, 18, 20, 45, 48, 52
Codex Beza, 62, 91
colophon, 98
Compte, August, 37n.
Coptic language, 14
Cox, Harvey, 37n.
creation 37, 68ff.
Cross, Frank L., 22, 38n., 40n.
Cybele, 29n.
Cyril of Jerusalem, 55n.

decad, 50, 98
De Catanzaro, C. J., 70
Dead Sea Scrolls, 18, 21, 80
Demi-urge, 27, 29, 43, 53, 76, 87, 98
demythologization, 93
Descent of Ishtar, 81
Deucalion, 87
Dialogue of the Saviour, 16
Diatesseron, 59, 60, 62
Discourse of Rheginos, 16, 33, 67
Discourse of Truth of Zoroaster, 17
Docetism, 35
Doresse, Jean, 12n., 15, 18, 19n., 20, 22, 41, 48n., 51n., 53, 64, 65, 66n., 67, 73n., 74n., 75, 75n., 77, 79, 80, 84n., 86n.
dualism, 25

Echamoth, Echmoth (see Achamoth), 66

Eleleth (Heleleth), 50, 74f.
emanations, 26, 98
Encratites, 77, 98
Ennead, 51, 98
Epiphanius, 30, 64, 73, 80, 85
Epistle of Flora, 41
Epistle of Eugnostos, 16, 59, 75, 79f.
Epistle (Apocryphon) *of James*, 16, 33, 34f., 48, 82, 83
Epistle of Peter to Philip, 17
Epistle (Discourse) of *Rheginos*, 16, 33, 36
Eucharist, 69f., 98
Eugnostos, 80
Eusebius, 77, 83
Evangelium Veritatis, see *Gospel of Truth*
Eve, 53, 73, 87
Exegesis of the Soul, 16, 72, 76f.

fall, 43
Fate, 28, 83
Filson, Floyd V., 44n.
First Father, 25, 26
Fitzmeyer, Joseph A., 55n.
flood, 47
Freedman, David Noel, 20n., 31n., 61n., 63, 66n., 92n.

Gartner, Bertil, 58n., 60, 63, 64, 66n.
Gilgamesh Epic, 74
Ginza, 74, 86, 87
Giversen, Soren, 20, 20n., 44, 46n., 48n., 53, 96
Gnosticism, 23-31
God, 25
Gold, Victor, R., 19, 22
Gospel of the Egyptians, 16, 61, 64n., 80, 82, 86, 91
Gospel of the Hebrews, 60, 61, 84
Gospel of Mary, 45
Gospel of Matthias, 77
Gospel of Philip, 16, 19, 20, 26, 38, 44, 45, 57, 64-71, 89, 90, 91n., 92

Gospel of Thomas, 15, 16, 19, 20, 21, 30, 31, 35, 38, 44, 45, 48, 55-63, 64, 65, 66, 67, 72, 82, 83, 92, 93

Gospel of Truth, 16, 19, 20, 24n., 25n., 28, 33, 37, 38-44, 47, 50, 65, 68, 72, 84, 89, 90

Grant, Robert M., 20n., 31, 31n., 54, 61, 63, 66n., 71, 92n., 93n.

Grobel, Kenrick, 19, 44

Guillaumont, Antoine, 20n., 56n., 63

hamartiology, 98

Harnack, Adolph, 23, 37

Harris, R. Laird, 44n.

Harvey, W. Wigan, 34

Heidel, Alexander, 74

Helmbold, Andrew K., 20n., 22, 54, 71, 90, 96

Hennecke, Edgar, 38n., 44

Heracleon, 29, 34, 36, 37

Hermetics, 17, 22, 98

Hippolytus, 30, 61, 69, 77

Holy Spirit, 69, (Paraclete) 83

Homer, 77

Homilies (Manichaean), 87

Hypostasis of the Archons, 16, 19, 20, 72-75, 76, 93

Infancy Gospel according to Thomas, 55

interpretation, 92, 93

Interpretation of Gnosis, 17

Irenaeus, 24, 26, 30, 34, 38, 40, 46, 48, 51, 59, 61, 67, 69, 70, 73

Isenberg, Wm. W., 44

Ishtar, 29n., 50

Isis, 29n.

Jahweh, 50

James, 34, 35, 45, 60, 82, 83, 84, 85

James, M. R., 55n.

Jerome, 84

Jesus, 35, 42, 43, 46, 48, 49, 53, 57, 58, 60, 77, 82, 83, 94

Johannesbuch, 74

John (disciple), 34, 45, 46, 48, 49, 51, 52, 53, 60, 83, 90

John of Parallos, 86

Jonas, Hans, 31, 40n., 94n.

Jubilees, 87

Jude, 85

Jung, Carl, 31, 32, 54

Jung Codex, 14, 16, 18, 19, 32-44

Justin Martyr, 29f., 63

Kasser, Rudolph, 48n.

Kephalia, 86

knowledge (*gnosis*), 24, 27, 35, 37, 43, 53, 68, 85, 87

Krause, Martin, 15n., 33n., 66n., 72n., 79n.

Labib, Pahor, 19, 33n., 72n., 79n.

Leipoldt, Johannes, 20n., 64n., 72n.

Leitzmann, Hans, 25

Longnecker, Richard, 92n.

Letter to Flora, 29, 80

Life of Adam and Eve, 86

MacRae, George W., 23n., 85n.

Malinine, Michael, 19n., 34n., 36n., 38n., 44

Mandaeans, 22, 23n., 29, 30, 31, 86, 87, 98

Manichaeans, 22, 25, 29, 31, 51n., 55, 81, 83, 86, 87, 98

Marcion, 42, 43, 59

Marcionites, 29, 98

Marcosians, 29, 40, 69, 70

Marcus, 29

Marcus, Ralph A., 27n.

Mareim, 84

Mariamme (Mariham), 58, 66, 82, 83

marriage, 66

Matthew, 58

Matthias, 34, 60, 66, 77

Merkeba, 75
Mina, Toga, 12, 18, 19n.
Montanists, 90, 98
Montefiore, Hugh, 63, 92n.

Naasenes, 25, 29, 60, 61, 77, 83
negative attributes, 26, 85
Nicolaitans, 77
Noah, 53, 73, 74, 87
Nock, Arthur Darby, 22, 40n.
Norea, 72, 74

Ogdoad, 76, 81, 99
On the Omega, 77
Origen, 28n., 40, 55, 58, 61, 77
Ophites, 29, 34, 60, 73
Oxyrhynchus papyri, 55f., 59, 60, 80

Paradise, 52, 68f., 73f.
Paraphrase of Shem, 17
Paul, 81
Pentad, 50
Peter, 34, 58, 60, 83
Philip, 34, 60, 64, 66, 67
Phoster, 87
Pistis Sophia (see Sophia), 16, 19, 75, 76
Pistis Sophia, 53, 59, 66, 73
Pleroma, 26f., 29, 36, 43, 50, 51, 66, 70, 75, 76, 84, 99
Plumley J. Martin, 72n., 78
Prayers of the Apostles, 16, 34
Pseudo-Clementine Recognitions, 63, 84
Pseudo-Tertullian, 40, 44
Ptolemaeus, Ptolemy, 41, 80
Puech, Henri-Charles, 14, 15, 18, 19n., 35, 37, 38n., 40n., 41n., 42n., 44, 47n., 55, 55n., 60, 60n., 64n., 66n., 67, 77n., 79, 80, 89n., 95
Pyrrha, 74

Quispel, Gilles, 19n., 32, 38n., 40, 40n., 44, 47, 62, 96

redemption, 27, 35, 41, 68ff., 95

Revelation of Adam, 85
Revelation of Dositheus, 17
Revelation of Messos, 17

Sabaoth, 51, 75, 76
Saclas, 27, 50
sacraments, 68f.
Sacred Book of the Great Invisible Spirit, 16, (also called Gospel of the Egyptians)
Salome, 58, 82
Salvation, 22, 25, 42, 48, 49, 53, 94
Samael, 27, 50, 73
Satan, 50
Save-Soderbergh, Torgny, 20n.
Schenke, Hans Martin, 20n., 48n., 64n., 66
Schmidt, Carl, 45, 46
Schoedel, Wm. R., 20
Second Clement, 83
Second Treatise of the Great Seth, 17, 86
Seth, 29, 50, 53, 74, 85, 86, 87
Sethians, 27, 29, 40, 73, 86, 87
Simon Magus, 67, 92
Simonians, 29, 99
Sithil, 86
Sophia, 26f., 29, 43, 50, 51, 52, 66, 70, 75, 83
Stephen, 85
syzygy, 26, 80, 99

Tatian, 30, 59, 62, 63
Teachings of Adam, 86
Teachings of Silvanus, 17
Tertullian, 40, 44, 93
Testament of Solomon, 51, 76
textual criticism, 91, 92
Theuda, 84
Thomas (disciple), 34, 58, 60, 66, 77
Thoughts of the Great Power, 17
Thunder: Perfect Mind, 18
Till, Walter, C., 14n., 15, 18n., 20, 44, 45, 47n., 54, 66n., 80n.

Traditions of Matthias, 77
Treatise on the Three Natures, 16, 34, 36f.
Tree of Knowledge, 52, 53, 73
Tree of Life, 52
Triple Discourse of the Triple Protennoia, 17
Turner, H. E. W., 92n., 93

Untitled Sethian Treatises, 16, 17, 75
Valentinus, 28, 34, 36, 38ff., 44
Valentinians, Valentinianism, 24, 25, 26, 27, 28f., 30, 33, 34, 35, 37, 38, 40, 41, 43, 47, 60, 65, 66, 67, 70, 83, 90n., 93n.
van Unnik, W. C., 22, 28n., 34, 35, 37, 40, 40n., 43, 55n., 60, 71, 89n.

Walther, C. F., 23
Western text, 62, 68, 89n., 91-92
Wilson, Robert L., 22, 23n., 31, 38n., 44, 47n., 63, 64n., 66n., 67, 68n., 71, 89n., 92n., 96
Wisdom of Jesus Christ, 16, 45, 48, 58, 66, 80
Wisdom of Solomon, 26

Yaldabaoth, 27, 29, 43, 50, 51, 52, 53, 73, 75, 76
Zodias, 50
Zoe, 72, 73, 75
Zoroastrianism, 87
Zosimos, 77

INDEX OF SCRIPTURE PASSAGES

Genesis — 27
Gen. 1:2 — 51
Gen. 1:26 — 51
Gen. 2 — 52
Gen. 2:23-24 — 51, 52
Gen. 3 — 29, 37
Gen. 6:2 — 74
Gen. 6:6 — 53

Exodus 7:3 — 95

Deut. 19:15 — 66

Psalms — 77

Proverbs — 26, 65

Isaiah — 84

Jeremiah 1:5 — 81

Hosea — 77

Matthew — 68, 84
Matt. 3:3ff. — 62
Matt. 5-7 — 62
Matt. 7:3-5 — 58
Matt. 9:15 — 91n.
Matt. 10:29 — 91n.
Matt. 12:32 — 58, 59, 62
Matt. 13 — 62
Matt. 15:14 — 58, 62
Matt. 16:1-4 — 91n.
Matt. 23:38 — 91n.
Matt. 26:61 — 57

Mark 3:9 — 53
Mark 4:13ff. — 62
Mark 9:34-50 — 57

Luke 3:32 — 91n.
Luke 6 — 62
Luke 6:41ff. — 62
Luke 6:16 — 84

Luke 10:1 — 91n.
Luke 10:17 — 91n.
Luke 11 — 62
Luke 12 — 62

John — 26, 36, 43, 68, 84, 89, 92
John 1:3 — 89n.
John 1:5 — 89n.
John 1:14 — 89n.
John 3:13 — 89n.
John 10:4 — 89n.
John 14:22 — 60
John 16:3 — 89n.
John 20:22 — 89n., 91n.
John 20:31 — 89n.

Acts 1:13 — 84
Acts 8:12f. — 67
Acts 17:25-30 — 43

Romans — 68
Rom. 1:18 — 3:20 — 41
Rom. 1:21 — 87

I Corinthians — 68
I Cor. 15 — 36
I Cor. 15:7 — 84

II Corinthians — 68
II Cor. 12:2 — 81

Galatians — 68, 84, 92
Gal. 1:15 — 81

Ephesians 5:21-32 — 70
Eph. 6:12 — 73

Philippians — 68

Colossians — 84

Hebrews — 68, 90
Heb. 1:5 — 90n.

Heb. 4:9 – 90n.
Heb. 4:11 – 90n.
Heb. 4:12 – 90n.
Heb. 5:5 – 90n.
Heb. 6:19f. – 90n.
Heb. 9:2ff. – 90n.
Heb. 9:10 – 90n.
Heb. 10:20 – 90n.
Heb. 10:26f. – 90n.
Heb. 10:39 – 90n.
Heb. 12:16-17 – 90n.
Heb. 12:18 – 90n.

I Peter – 68

II Peter – 90, 91
II Peter 1:17 – 91n.
II Peter 2:2 – 91n.
II Peter 2:4-5 – 91n.

I John – 68

Revelation – 47, 89, 90
Rev. 1 – 49
Rev. 1:19 – 90
Rev. 12:6 – 87